FINAL ANSWER

"You asked, God Answered"

John Marshall

Copyright © 2003 by John Marshall
Final Answer
by John Marshall

Printed in the United States of America
ISBN 0974069353

All rights reserved. This book or parts thereof may not be reproduced in any form, stored in a retrieval system, or transmitted in any form by any means—electronic, mechanical, photocopy, recording, or otherwise—without prior written permission of the publisher, except as provided by United States copyright law.

Unless otherwise quoted, all Scripture quotations are from the New American Standard Version of the Bible. Copyright © 1960, 1962, 1963, 1968, 1971, 1972, 1973, 1975, 1977, 1995 by the Lockman Foundation, a Corporation Not for Profit.
Scripture quotations marked KJV are from the King James Version of the Bible.

Dedication

DI dedicate this book to our four children, Terrence, Marrkus, Jondreia, and Johnathan. Each of them is as diverse and divergent as the questions of this book. But, just as I learned something as I responded to each of the questions of this book, I also learned something as I responded to each of my children.

For a long time, I thought that God gave parents to the children so that the children could learn about life. But now, I am totally convinced that God gave children to parents so that parents could learn about life. Terrence, Marrkus, Jondreia, and Johnathan, you are my heart. Indeed, you are the greatest. May God forever smile favorably upon you, yours and all of your efforts.

TABLE OF CONTENTS

Introduction 11

Bible 13
- Word of God
- Standard of Authority
- Guide for Humanity

God 27
- Presence of God
- Power of God
- Relationship of God

Jesus Christ 37
- Description of Jesus
- Relation to God
- Significance of the Crucifixion

Holy Spirit 45
- Promise of the Holy Spirit
- Function of the Holy Spirit
- Gift of the Holy Spirit

Salvation 55
- Promise of Salvation
- Steps to Salvation
- Key factors of Salvation

Church 61
- Origin of the Church
- Commands for the Church
- Worship in the Church

Sabbath 69
- Significance of the Sabbath
- First Sabbath Observance
- The Sabbath Versus Sunday

Prayer 83
- Model of Prayer
- Response from Prayer
- Reaction to God

Forgiveness 89
- Requirements of Forgiveness
- Formula for Forgiveness
- Proof of Forgiveness

Sin **101**
- Meaning of Sin
- Ranking of Sin
- God's Response to Sin

Death **119**
- What is Death?
- Death for the Wicked
- Death for the Righteous

Marriage. **123**
- Basis for Marriage
- Preparation for Marriage
- Conflicts with Marriage

Divorce. **135**
- Clarification of the Law
- About Divorce
- Cost of Divorce

Things That You Should Do **145**

INTRODUCTION

For the past five years, I have hosted Call & Ask. Call & Ask is a local and national question and answer telecast. Definitely, thousands have watched and listen while hundreds have watched and asked. Hopefully all who watched have learned. The questions and answers within Final Answer came from my dialogue with those callers.

Jesus answered questions. Sometimes He answered directly (Matthew 9:14-17). Sometimes He answered indirectly (Matthew 22:23-27). At times instead of providing the information they thought they wanted, He provided the information, He knew they needed (John 4:7-26). Occasionally Jesus initiated the discussion and invited them to discover their answers for themselves (John 1:38-39).

In all the instances with Jesus, the profundity of God shone forth. Through the answers Jesus gave all could learn. Hopefully, through the answers that I have given many have learned. I pray that you who will read these answers will likewise also learn.

James declared, "...You do not have because you do not ask" (James 4:2). Jesus recommended, "Ask, and it will be given to you; seek and you will find; knock, and it will be opened to you" (Matthew 7:7). May God forever position you for prosperity because you have been inquisitive enough to read.

BIBLE

Over a period of about sixteen-hundred years, some forty different writers from various cultural and educational backgrounds, recorded the Bible. Yet, no Bible writer ever disputed what another writer wrote. In spite of many diversities, the Bible uniformly describes: 1) the personality and character of God (Exodus 34:6; Romans 2:4), 2) the personality and character of humankind (Jeremiah 17:9; Romans 1:21-32), 3) the human need for salvation (Exodus 32:32; Matthew 6:12-15; Luke 5:21-24), and 4) the anticipation and coming of a savior (Deuteronomy 18:15-19; Acts 3:22–23). *Without divine revelation, the human mind was and is incapable of producing the Bible.*

The first original handwritten copy of each book of the Bible was an "autograph copy." The autograph copy of each Old Testament book was written in the Hebrew language. From these autograph copies, scribes made "manuscript copies" in the Hebrew language and circulated them among the people.

In the Second Century BC, scribes translated manuscript copies into the Greek language and called it the "Septuagint." Frequently, Jesus quoted from the Septuagint and even referred to its divisions (Matthew 22:32; Luke 24:44).

The autograph copy of each New Testament book was written in the Greek language and circulated them among the early church. New Testament textual critics have discovered some five-thousand manuscripts in different places throughout the Ancient World.

Scholars have diligently compared manuscript copies and translated them into the English language. Basically, two types of translations exist: the dynamic equivalence and formal equivalence. The dynamic equivalence is an attempt to translate the exact thought while the formal equivalence is an attempt to translate the exact word.

The New International Version (NIV) is a dynamic equivalence. The New American Standard Version (NASB) and the King James Version (KJV) are formal equivalence. Scholarly translations are in existence.

If scholars had never translated the Old Testament from the Hebrew language and the New Testament from the Greek language into the English language, you would need to learn both the Hebrew and Greek languages before you could study the Word of God. You should thank God for reliable translations; they greatly assist your understanding of God's Word.

In Great Britain during the reign of King James (1604–1611), fifty-four Bible scholars translated the King James Version of the Bible. It was given this title *not* because King James decided what the resulting translation would be, but because it was translated during his reign and at his encouraging.

Initially, the writing of the Bible embraced the culture of human beings who lived on the continents of Africa, Asia and Europe. The Eunuch came from Ethiopia on the continent of Africa (Acts 8:27). While, the disputing disciples came from Jerusalem on the continent of Asia (Acts 15:1-4). The apostle Paul left Athens and went to Corinth both are on the continent of Europe (Acts 18:1). In spite of being initially addressed to only three different continents, the scripture relates and applies to all human beings over the entire world.

The Old Testament

The Bible is divided into two "testaments." The first testament is the Old Testament which contains thirty-nine books. These books are not arranged in chronological order.

It contains five books of Law often called the Pentateuch (Genesis, Exodus, Leviticus, Numbers and Deuteronomy). Laws are generally written in exact terminology with little or no symbolic and figurative language. We can expect the language of these five books to be exact and specific. For example observe the exactness: *"tenth day," "fourteenth day"* (Exodus 12:3-6).

It contains twelve books of History (Joshua, Judges, Ruth, First Samuel, Second Samuel, First Kings, Second Kings, First Chronicles, Second Chronicles, Ezra, Nehemiah and Esther). These books contain a historical record of the Israelites wandering in the desert, and the entering and dwelling in the Promised Land.

It contains five books of Wisdom Literature often called Poetry (Job, Psalms, Proverbs, Ecclesiastes and Song of Solomon). Poetry is usually written in highly figurative and symbolic language. For example observe the figurativeness: *paths of righteousness, shadow of death* (Psalm 23:1-6).

It contains seventeen books of Prophecy. Books of prophecy "foretold" or predicted future events, *"It will come about after this…"* (Joel 2:28-32). Also, books of prophecy "forth told" or explained the predicted events once they began to occur, *"but this is what was spoken of through the prophet Joel…"* (Acts 2:16-21). The prophecy in Joel "foretells" what the prophecy in Acts "forth tells."

Five of the prophetic books are called Major Prophets, simply because of their long length not because of importance (Isaiah, Jeremiah, Lamentations, Ezekiel and Daniel). While, twelve of the prophetic books are called Minor Prophets, simply because of their short length not because of lack of importance (Hosea, Joel, Amos, Obadiah, Jonah, Micah, Nahum, Habakkuk, Zephaniah, Haggai, Zechariah, and Malachi).

The New Testament

The second testament is the New Testament. It contains twenty-seven books. These books are neither arranged in chronological order nor order of importance. Sometimes they are arranged according to length.

It contains four Gospels, which are historical narratives of the earthly life of Jesus Christ (Matthew, Mark, Luke, and John). These books contain information from the time shortly before the birth of Jesus until shortly after His death.

It contains a single book of History, (Acts) the historical narrative of where and how Christianity began and grew. This book contains messages preached directly to and for those who had not become disciples of Christ. Therefore, the book of Acts more directly and precisely answers the question, "What must I do to become saved, forgiven of sin?"

It contains twenty-one Letters. Nine letters were written to churches (Romans, First Corinthians, Second Corinthians, Galatians, Ephesians, Philippians, Colossians, First Thessalonians, and Second Thessalonians).

Twelve letters were written to individuals (First Timothy, Second Timothy, Titus, Philemon, Hebrews, James, First Peter, Second Peter, First John, Second John, Third John, and Jude). Romans through Thessalonians were named for the city where the churches were located. First Timothy through Philemon bears the name of the person to whom the letter was addressed. James through

Jude bears the name of the one who wrote the letter.

Finally, it contains one book of Prophecy (Revelation).

Q What makes you think the Bible is the Word of God?

A There is much evidence for the Bible being the Word of God. I believe that the Bible is the Word of God because of the accuracy of its fulfilled prophecy. The Old Testament was written before Jesus was ever born. The Old Testament contains prophecies concerning His birthplace (Micah 5:1-2); the fact of His virgin birth (Isaiah 7:14); that He would be rejected by His own people (Isaiah 53:3); that He would be betrayed by a close friend (Isaiah 41:9); and that He would rise from the dead (Psalms 16:10, 49:15).

Men who walked with, ate with, and learned from Jesus wrote the New Testament. He fulfilled the Old Testament prophecies. *"If the Bible is not inspired from God, then why does it contain so many fulfilled prophecies?"*

Only God knows the future, has power over it, and can look into it to tell us exactly what will happen. The Bible contains the divine fingerprints of God's fulfilled prophecy!

Q What is our standard of authority?

A The message of scripture is our standard of authority. The word "authority" means "the right to command or act." Therefore, authority in religion would mean the right to command or act religiously. Jeremiah said, *"I know, O Lord, that a man's way is not in himself; Nor is it in a man who walks to direct his steps"* (Jeremiah 10:23). The human mind is inadequate as an ultimate standard of authority. God calls a man a "fool" who would reject the divine standard of authority and trust in his own heart (Proverbs 28:26).

After Christ arose from the dead, he gave the great commission, *"...All authority has been given to me in heaven and on earth"* (Matthew 28:18). Our authority in religion is Christ. God has acknowledged him publicly as His Son (Matthew 3:13-17). He is now our mediator and God's spokesman for the new covenant (Hebrews 1:1).

The Bible is man's only true creed and the New Testament our only code of law in matters of religion. Herein, God has given us all things necessary for life and godliness (2 Peter 1:3-4). The Scriptures furnish us completely unto all good works (2 Timothy 3:15-17). We are commanded not to go beyond the things that are written (1 Corinthians 4:6). Nothing may be added to, or taken from, this established standard of authority (Revelation 22:18-19). We must do as Paul urged Timothy, to rightly handle the word of truth (2 Timothy 2:15).

"All Scripture is inspired by God" (2 Timothy 3:15-17). The things Paul wrote were "the commandments of the Lord" (1 Corinthians 14:37).

He wrote to Timothy that he might know how to live right. These writings in the New Testament were for us so that we might believe in Christ and accept the truth. God has given these writings to keep us from sin; and that we might know the certainty of the truth of Christianity and as Christians we might have eternal life (I John 5:13).

Q *How can the Bible with all of its human element be authoritative?*

A Whatever the occasion or their method of writing, the authors of Scripture were "so moved by the Holy Spirit" that they communicated what God intended. *"So we have the prophetic word made more sure, to which you do well to pay attention as to a lamp shining in a dark place, until the day dawns and the morning star arises in your hearts. But know this first of all, that no prophecy of Scripture is a matter of one's own interpretation, for no prophecy was ever made by an act of human will, but men moved by the Holy Spirit spoke from God"* (2 Peter 1:19-21).

Scripture did not come from the Biblical writers. Scripture came to the Biblical writers. God gave them divine competence in writing. This competence enabled them to express adequately the revelatory matters they wanted to communicate.

God deposited within the thoughts of men His words and ideas (1 Corinthians 2:6-13;

Ephesians 3:1-5; Jeremiah 36:1-2, 4, 8, 17-18, 23, 27-32; 2 Peter 1:20-21).

The U.S. Constitution is purely a human production; yet, it is the final authority. The Bible does have a divine element; we ought to give it much more credibility than we do the U.S. Constitution.

Q *Is the Bible adequate to govern us in such complex times as we now live? Must we really restrict ourselves to the principles of Scripture?*

A Our complex times have not caught God off guard nor by surprise. Yes, the Bible is adequate to govern us. *"You, however, continue in the things you have learned and become convinced of, knowing from whom you have learned them and that from childhood you have known the sacred writings which are able to give you the wisdom that leads to salvation through faith which is in Christ Jesus. All Scripture is inspired by God and profitable for teaching, for reproof, for correction, for training in righteousness; so that the man of God may be adequate, equipped for every good work"* (2 Timothy 3:14-17).

Yes, we must restrict ourselves to principles of Scripture. *"Now these things, brethren, I have figuratively applied to myself and Apollos for your sakes, so that in us you may learn not to exceed what is written, so that no one of you will become arrogant in behalf of one against the other"* (1 Corinthians 4:6).

Q Why should we believe that the New Testament is reliable?

A It is a historical book that is historically accurate. It is recorded by eyewitnesses and researched among eyewitnesses (Luke 1:1-4). None of its facts are proven to be false.

The New Testament recorded the history of certain persons, events, times, places, and cultures. Those who first received it accepted it as an accurate report. They could have invalidated its claims if it had been inaccurate for many of those about whom it was written were still alive (1 Corinthians 15:1-4).

Q Of the four gospels, which account is true?

A All are true. Each provides different information to a different audience for a different purpose. Compare:

Mark 14:47—Someone cut off the ear of the slave of the high priest. *"But one of those who stood by drew his sword, and struck the slave of the high priest and cut off his ear"*.

Matthew 26:51—Someone with Jesus cut off the ear of the slave of the high priest. *"And behold, one of those who were with Jesus reached and drew out his sword, and struck the slave of the high priest and cut off his ear"*.

Luke 22:50—Someone cut of the right ear of the slave of the high priest. *"And one of them struck the slave of the high priest and cut off his right ear"*.

John 18:10—Peter cut off Malchus's ear. *"Simon Peter then, having a sword, drew it and struck the high priest's slave, and cut off his right ear; and the slave's name was Malchus"*.

Q *Is reading the Bible all I need to do, or should I read the history of Christianity as well?*

A The Bible alone is adequate. *"All Scripture is inspired by God and profitable for teaching, for reproof, for correction, for training in righteousness; so that the man of God may be adequate, equipped for every good work"* (2 Timothy 3:15-17).

Q *How can we all understand the Bible alike?*

A Ordinary people can understand the Bible. The Bible is understandable (2 Timothy 3:14-17). It is the will of the Lord for us to understand it alike (1 Corinthians 1:10).

Validate your understanding totally by the Bible. Teach only validated truths that can be document by what is written (1 Corinthians 4:6). In every church, teach only what is written (1 Corinthians 4:17). Have no fellowship with those who insist on teaching otherwise (Galatians 1:6-9; 2 John 9-11).

Q *Who should interpret Scripture, the church, preacher, or each individual?*

A The Ethiopian read the Scriptures, but understood not (Acts 8:25-31). What would have been different if he had believed continually that Isaiah was talking about himself (Acts 8:34)?

The disciples of Jesus heard him, but understood not (Matthew 16:5-12). What would have been different if the disciples had believed that Jesus was only talking about bread to eat?

One can misunderstand the Scriptures and cause his own ruin (2 Peter 3:14-17). Often we need help to understand the word of God.

The author of each statement in Scripture had an intended meaning in his mind for the statements that he said or wrote. Readers are not entitled to their own opinion about the Scriptures but are entitled to the opinion of the author. Neither the church, preacher nor each individual should interpret scripture contrary to the author's original intended meaning (1 Corinthians 4:6). Let the precepts, principles and precedents within Scripture interpret for us. Using our God-given rational reasoning ability, we can draw correct conclusion from the Bible (John 8:31-32, 2 Timothy 3:14-15).

Q *What does the Bible say about eternal life?*

A There are two senses in which this is used. First, Christians possess eternal life (1 John 5:13), yet we are not in heaven. Though we are still in our mortal bodies and we still sin, by faith we are saved (Romans 4:5; Ephesians 2:8-9) and possess eternal life as a free gift from God (Romans 6:23). Second, eternal life will reach its final state at the resurrection of the believers when Christ returns to earth to claim His church. It is then that eternal life will begin in its complete manifestation. We will no longer sin (1 Thessalonians 4:17).

Q Does the Bible contain scientific errors and scientifically erroneous concepts?
A The Bible is not a book of science, but when it speaks scientifically, it is scientifically accurate (Genesis 1:1-12; 21; 24-25).

Q How do the Dead Sea Scrolls affect the Bible? Did the writers of the Bible pick and choose what they wrote? Are the scrolls missing books of the Bible?
A The Dead Sea Scrolls do not negatively affect the Bible. No, nothing in the Dead Sea Scrolls contradicts or adds distinctively different information. For the most part, the Dead Sea Scrolls just confirm what is in Scripture.

Q Where is God?
A The apostle Paul described Jehovah as the God who comforts during all afflictions. *"Blessed be the God and Father of our Lord Jesus Christ, the Father of mercies and God of all comfort, who*

comforts us in all our affliction so that we will be able to comfort those who are in any affliction with the comfort with which we ourselves are comforted by God" (2 Corinthians 1:3-4). To comfort was to stand beside, console and/or encourage. The word "afflictions" described a pressing together, oppression and/or suffering.

God remains near to us. *"and He made from one man every nation of mankind to live on all the face of the earth, having determined their appointed times and the boundaries of their habitation, that they would seek God, if perhaps they might grope for Him and find Him, though He is not far from each one of us; for in Him we live and move and exist, as even some of your own poets have said, 'For we also are His children"* (Acts 17:26-28).

God remains near to console and encourage us. God remains near to encourage and console us throughout the duration of our sufferings. *"At my first defense no one supported me, but all deserted me; may it not be counted against them. But the Lord stood with me and strengthened me, so that through me the proclamation might be fully accomplished, and that all the Gentiles might hear; and I was rescued out of the lion's mouth"* (2 Timothy 4:14-18).

GOD

God is that being which no one or no thing greater can be conceived. God is superior or more perfect than all else. He is the being in which all authority and truth resides.

There is only one true God, Who has revealed Himself as the eternal, self-existent One (Deuteronomy 6:4, Isaiah 43:10-13). To be self-existent means that His existence depends upon no one other than Himself. He came into existence by His own power and He remains in existence by His own power. As the eternal One, He has and will always exist.

God is infinite and sovereign to the universe. To be infinite is to be exceedingly immense and inexhaustible without limits. To be sovereign is to be the greatest supreme authority.

Attributes of God

"Elohim." "El" was an ancient Hebrew prefix meaning God. Elohim expresses the might of the creator as the sustainer of this universe. (Genesis 1:1; Acts 17:24; Hebrews 3:4). God is the creator of all, everything in the vast universe. He is the creator of man, earth and everything on earth. Not only is God creative, but He is administrative in nature. He desires to govern His creation.

He created natural laws such as the law of gravity and the laws of condensation and evaporation (Amos 5:8; 9:6; Isaiah 55:8-10; Psalms 137:7; Jeremiah 10:13, 51:16). As Elohim, we understand Him as a God who can do all that He wills to do.

"El Shaddai." El Shaddai expresses His almightiness and His self-sufficiency (Philippians 4:19; 2 Corinthians 3:5; Genesis 17:1).

"Jehovah." Jehovah expresses His consistency and faithfulness to His covenanted promises (Titus 1:2; Hebrews 6:13-18). As Jehovah, God is unchangeable.

Q Why should we believe that the universe was created by God?

A Answering these two questions will help.

(1) Who put it here? The sun, stars, moon and other heavenly bodies—no accident causes something of this magnitude. Somebody put it here.

(2) Who put it here like this? The sun, stars, moon and other heavenly bodies are precisely arranged. They have at least a triple synchroniza-

tion: annually, seasonally (winter, spring, summer and fall) and daily rotation arrangement. This is no accident. Somebody put it here like this. Only the intelligence and power ascribed to God can account for the existence of the universe.

Q ***Does God send us signs? How can we determine if they are from God or Satan?***

A The resurrection of Jesus is our greatest sign. *"The Jews then said to Him, What sign do You show us as your authority for doing these things? Jesus answered them, Destroy this temple, and in three days, I will raise it up. The Jews then said, It took forty-six years to build this temple, and will You raise it up in three days? But He was speaking of the temple of His body. So when He was raised from the dead, His disciples remembered that He said this; and they believed the Scripture and the word which Jesus had spoken"* (John 2:18-22).

God expects us to know and believe because we hear His written Word, not because we see a sign. *"But Thomas, one of the twelve, called Didymus, was not with them when Jesus came. So the other disciples were saying to him, "We have seen the Lord!" But he said to them, "Unless I see in His hands the imprint of the nails, and put my finger into the place of the nails, and put my hand into His side, I will not believe. After eight days His disciples were again inside, and Thomas with them. Jesus came, the doors hav-*

ing been shut, and stood in their midst and said, Peace be with you. Then He said to Thomas, Reach here with your finger, and see My hands; and reach here your hand and put it into My side; and do not be unbelieving, but believing. Thomas answered and said to Him, My Lord and my God! Jesus said to him, Because you have seen Me, have you believed? Blessed are they who did not see, and yet believed. Therefore many other signs Jesus also performed in the presence of the disciples, which are not written in this book; but these have been written so that you may believe that Jesus is the Christ, the Son of God; and that believing you may have life in His name" (John 20:24-31).

Q *How can I be sure that I am hearing the voice of God and not the voice of the devil?*

A God communicates more clearly through His written Word (Luke 10:25-26; 1 Timothy 3:14-15; 2 Timothy 3:16-17). Any thought, intuition, urge or preference that violates His written Word cannot be the voice of God, but of Satan.

Q *Is God still doing miracles today?*

A Do we dare question the power of God today? Does He not now have the same eternal, unlimited power as always? Do we presume to limit the power of God in affirming that no miracles occur today? The answer to these questions is an emphatic "no"!

What God is able to do and what He wills to do are completely different issues. God once created man from the dust, and woman from man's rib. He once parted the Red Sea to permit the escape of Israel from Egypt and rained manna from heaven upon them. He provided quail in the wilderness and water from the rock to supply Israel's needs. He gave commandments inscribed on stone with His finger. He once caused His Son to be born of a virgin. Jesus performed numerous miracles ranging from feeding the hungry to raising the dead. None of these miracles are being witnessed in our time. To say that miracles do not happen as they once did is not to entertain doubts or define limits of divine power. It is merely to raise the question of what His will is for our day.

The term "miracle" has been subjected to indiscriminate usage in our time. Almost anything unusual is incorrectly styled a "miracle." Three different Greek words are used for miracle. All three words are used in such passages as (Acts 2:22; 2 Corinthians 12:12; Hebrews 2:4).

God is not performing miracles for the purpose that He did during the days of the apostles (Hebrews 2:3-4). In short, a miracle was something that was done contrary to the laws of nature to prove that God was working through the one who could demonstrate the power. It does not just mean something merely unusual, strange, or out of the ordinary.

Miracles were never performed just to prolong life or eliminate human suffering universally. Jesus could have raised all the dead, but He did not; He could have healed all the sick, but He did not. Paul healed many, but did not heal Timothy and Trophimus (1 Timothy 5:23; 2 Timothy 4:20). All who were delivered from sickness and suffering did eventually die.

All healing is divine. Men may cut, saw, and sew, but only God heals. We have a right to think of Him as a healer (Exodus 15:26). His Spirit dwells within us and we should ask Him to meet our needs. But professional divine healers, with their purported gift of healing, are something entirely different. The gift of healing was a sign that introduced, corroborated and authenticated the gospel message before the complete New Testament was written (Acts 10:38; 4:30). When the Word with its authority was written, the appeal is no longer to the "signs" but to what's written (1 Corinthians 4:6; 2 Timothy 3:16-17).

Q Who should determine what our moral standard should be?

A Morality is a code of ethics, expressions of right and wrong behavior. There are four options:

(1) Intuition—inherently knows. If so, this question would never be asked. We could never criticize the behavior of another.

(2) Consequences—one would never know the consequences of his behavior until it was too late. Even then consequences may differ from one occasion to another occasion.

(3) Society or Majority—the majority determines what is right or wrong. What criteria will be used to determine what is right and wrong?

(4) God the Creator—provides the best standard for our moral conduct (2 Timothy 3:16-17).

Q *When you pray to God in search of His Word and His answer, how do you know without a doubt that God is listening? How do you get in a position to hear Him?*

A Learn the ways of God from Scripture. Believe the report of Scripture and trust God to do what He said He will do. If you are numbered among the righteous, you can know that God is listening because He promises to hear and respond to the prayers of His children (1 Peter 3:12). But, prayer alone is inadequate, you must do the will of God (1 Peter 3:10-11).

Q *Can you help me to understand the vision that God gave to me?*

A Why do you think that the vision was of God (Jeremiah 23:16)? When God gave visions to His people, they always understood and did not have to seek a human explanation (Genesis 15:1-5; Numbers 12:6-7; 1 Samuel 3; 2 Samuel 7; 1 Chronicles 17; Daniel 8:15; Acts 9:10; 10:3; 16:9-10; 18:9). When God gave visions to those who were not His people, they never understood and had to seek a human explanation (Genesis 41:1-13, Daniel 4:4-18). Why would God give you a vision and require someone who did not receive the vision to interpret it?

Q When you know that you have a calling from God on your life, what are the things you need to do to find out what it is?

A How do you know that you have a calling from God? The same way you know that you have a calling; you should know what the calling is.

When God called, He always called clearly (Luke 5:10-11; Acts 9:5-19). Now, God calls and assigns through the gospel (2 Thessalonians 2:14, 1 Peter 4:10-11). Do what it says and all else will become crystal clear.

Q Does God ever change his mind?
A Yes, read Exodus 32:1-14.

Q How may we ever be assured that we are right with God since our lives are always imperfect and none of us is without sin?

A By the love, mercy and grace of God, He saved us (Ephesians 2:8-9). By His discipline (1 Peter 1:5-9; Hebrews 12:3-11) and by His directions, God keeps us saved (2 Peter 1:1-11, 1 John 5:11-13).

Q What about rewards?

A God rewards based upon our willingness to:

(1) serve Him (1 Corinthians 3:5-8, 2 Corinthians 5:10, Revelation 22:12, 2 John 8)

(2) suffer for Him (Matthew 5:11-12, 2 Timothy 2:11-12, Hebrews 11:24-26, 1 Peter 4:12-19)

Jesus Christ

Jesus startled His friends and angered His enemies by referring to God as His Father (Matthew 27:43). He took His own directions from God, pointed others to God, and depended on God for all His needs—including His resurrection victory over death (John 5:19, 30; 17:3-4; Luke 23:46; Hebrews 5:7).

At the same time, Jesus claimed a unique oneness with the Father (John 14:8-11; 17:3-5, 20-23), a claim that would be quite blasphemous were it not true (Matthew 26:63-65).

Names for Jesus from Scripture

Jesus is the *Word* (John 1:1; 14). Here "Word" is translated from the Greek word *logos*. We obtain our English word *logo* from this Greek word *Logos*. Logos (the Word) was a visible demonstration of a concept. In other words, Jesus visibly demonstrated the concept of God. Hebrews 1:8 refers to Jesus as God.

In the beginning the "Word" existed. The "Word" was Jesus. The "Word" existed before He was born into the world as Jesus the Son of God (John 1:1). The "Word" was with God and also was God (John 1:1). In the beginning before the "Word" was born into the world as the Son of God and before there existed Father and Son they existed as God. Long before anything else existed, they (God and the "Word") existed as supreme beings who had always existed. Before anything else came into existence there was God and the Word. All things were made by the Word (John 1:3, Ephesians 3:9).

Jesus is *Lord* (Acts 2:36). He is the *Wonderful Counselor* (Isaiah 9:6). As the wonderful counselor He counsels and admonishes (Matthew 11:28-30; 18:1-6).

Jesus is the *Mighty God* (Isaiah 9:6). As the mighty God He displays His strength (Matthew 28:18; Colossians 1:13-18).

Jesus is the *Everlasting Father* or the *father of eternity* (Isaiah 9:6). As the *Everlasting Father*, His duration is eternal (1 Corinthians 15:20-26; Revelation 1:5-8).

Jesus is the Prince of Peace. As the prince of peace, He reconciles mankind to

God. To reconcile is to reestablish favorable relationship (Ephesians 1:2; 2:11-16).

Q *Where in the Scripture does it say that the Lord has wooly hair and skin of bronze?*

A "I kept looking until thrones were set up, And the Ancient of Days took His seat; His vesture was like white snow And the hair of His head like pure wool. His throne was ablaze with flames, its wheels were a burning fire" (Daniel 7:9).

"His head and His hair were white like white wool, like snow; and His eyes were like a flame of fire. His feet were like burnished bronze, when it has been made to glow in a furnace, and His voice was like the sound of many waters" (Revelation 1:14-15).

Q *In respect to the Scripture reference of Deuteronomy 24:15-16, why did Jesus die for someone else (our) sins?*

A That text states, "You shall give him his wages on his day before the sun sets, for he is poor and sets his heart on it; so that he will not cry against you to the Lord and it become sin in you. Fathers shall not be put to death for their sons, nor shall sons be put to death for their fathers; everyone shall be put to death for his own sin" (Deuteronomy 24:15-16).

Sin demanded the death of the sinner, "The Lord God commanded the man, saying, *"From any tree of the garden you may eat freely; but from the tree of the knowledge of good and evil you shall not eat, for in the day that you eat from it you will surely die."* (Genesis 2:16-17). God sent His Son to become the propitiation (adequate substitute) for the sins of the whole world.

In Deuteronomy the context denotes that the death of any other father serves no value for the sins of the child. Only the death of Jesus provides intrinsic value. Sin demanded the death of an innocent one. All fathers are guilty themselves.

Q Can I believe in Jesus and yet not believe that the world was supernaturally created?

A No. Jesus Christ authenticated the Biblical record of the creation, *"But Jesus said to them, Because of your hardness of heart he wrote you this commandment. But from the beginning of creation, God made them male and female"* (Mark 10:5-6). *"For those days will be a time of tribulation such as has not occurred since the beginning of the creation which God created until now, and never will"* (Mark 13:19). *"Some Pharisees came to Jesus, testing Him and asking, Is it lawful for a man to divorce his wife for any reason at all? And He answered and said, "Have you not read that He who created them from the beginning made them male and female"* (Matthew 19:3-4). Jesus knew about and participated in the creation, *"He is the image of the invisible God, the firstborn of all creation. For by Him all things were created, both in the heavens and on earth, visible and invisible, whether thrones or dominions or rulers or authorities all things have been created through Him and for*

Him. He is before all things, and in Him all things hold together. He is also head of the body, the church; and He is the beginning, the firstborn from the dead, so that He Himself will come to have first place in everything" (Colossians 1:15-19, Genesis 1:26).

If Jesus is the Son of God, He must speak only truth. If He spoke error when he spoke favorably for the creation, He cannot be the Son of God. He is the Son of God and He did speak truth about the creation.

Q What does John 5:39-40 mean?

A *"You search the Scriptures because you think that in them you have eternal life; it is these that testify about Me; and you are unwilling to come to Me so that you may have life"* (John 5:39-40). The Jews who searched the Scriptures thought they had gained eternal life for their much study. Jesus said obviously you have searched inadequately for the very Scriptures that you search testify of Me, the one who gives eternal life. They refused to come to the one to whom the Scriptures testified.

Q Is Jesus really the Son of God?

A The term Son of God was a designation denoting the deity or divinity of Jesus Christ (Matthew 16:16-17). Scripture emphatically calls Jesus the Son of God (Luke 1:35; John 3:16; Romans 1:1-4).

Q **When Jesus was on the cross and cried out "Lord why has thou forsake me, did He lose His faith?**

A   No. This is a quote from Psalm 22. Frequently a portion of the Psalm would be quoted while referring to the whole Psalm. When we examine the whole context and content of this Psalm, it indicates that rather than being a fearful statement this indicated a reliance on God rather than a lack of trust.

Read carefully (Matthew 26:42). Jesus prayed to God who was able to save Him from death (Hebrews 5:7). But how can we say that Jesus' prayer was answered (heard) if He prayed to avoid death, for certainly He died on the cross? "Save him FROM death" can just as well be translated "save him OUT OF death." Jesus did not pray to avoid death—He had already set His face to the destiny appointed for Him (John 12:27-28; Isaiah. 50:5-10). He prayed that, after He died, God would "save Him out of death" by raising Him to life again. God heard this prayer of His pious Son and did exactly what His Son asked.

This fits the Biblical usage of the expression "the cup," which Jesus prayed would "pass from" Him. Throughout the Old Testament, God's punishment against sin is pictured as a "cup" which God Himself mixes and hands to the person to be punished, who must "drink" it (Isaiah 51:17, 22-23; Jeremiah. 25:15-38).

Sometimes a person drinks God's cup and it sends them reeling, but God then takes the cup back from their hand and they recover. Sometimes, however, God does not take the cup back—and the person who drinks it falls to the ground and never rises again (Jeremiah 25:27).

Jesus will drink the cup, for He knows that is God's will (Matthew 26:42). But, He knows also that God will raise Him from the dead (John 10:17-18).

Jesus drank the cup and died. But God took the cup back from Jesus' hand—he saved Him out of death—and Jesus rose again in vindication of His own faith and of God's faithfulness. "Let this cup pass from me," Jesus prayed. And it did! But because Jesus first drank THAT cup, we do not have to drink it. Instead, Jesus hands us the cup of the new covenant to drink—a cup, which attests that we are forgiven (Matthew 26:27-28).

Q *Is belief in the flood essential to Christianity?*
A Yes. To deny the flood is to deny the deity of Jesus (Matthew 24:37-38, Luke 17:26-27). If Jesus is the Son of God, He must speak only truth. He based several fundamental truths upon the fact of the flood. If He erred concerning His knowledge of the flood, He could not be the Son of God. He is the Son of God, He spoke truth about the flood. He did not err.

Holy Spirit

In contrast to what it says about the Father and the Son, Scripture says little about the Holy Spirit Himself. However, it does reveal His work.

Scripture provides much information about the Father: His qualities, purpose, loves, and role in salvation. It details even more about the Son: His volunteering to come and do the Father's will, involvements in becoming a man, earthly ministry, present activity and imminent return. But we do not have this sort of detail about the Holy Spirit.

We read of the Gospel of God (Romans 1:1; 15:16; 2 Corinthians 11:7; 1 Thessalonians 2:2,8,9; 1 Peter 4:17) and the Gospel of Christ (Romans 1:16; 15:19, 29; 1 Corinthians 9:12; 2 Corinthians 4:4; Philippians 1:27). Yet, we never read of the Gospel of the Spirit.

Scripture repeatedly refers to holy men preaching Christ, but we don't read of men preaching the Spirit. The Holy Spirit did not come to upstage the Savior (John 13-14). Scripture says that men of God preached the kingdom (Acts 8:12), repentance and forgiveness of sins (Luke 24:47), and the cross of Christ (1 Corinthians 1:21-23). Never did men of God preach the Spirit.

The Holy Spirit was never the subject of their preaching, but rather He was the worker who brought the preaching home to the heart, convicting and persuading men of the truth (John 16:7-11). The indwelling of the Spirit is not an end within itself—it is what He *does* that is the point.

Uninformed people have made *receiving* the Spirit the point. The Word of God makes *what He does within our hearts* the point.

God now gives the Holy Spirit to those who obey Him (Acts 5:32; Romans 5:5; 1 Corinthians 6:19). Notice the relationship of the Holy Spirit to obedience. This refers to our beginning obedience to the Gospel (Acts 2:38). Jesus called it believing and being baptized (Mark 16:16). Paul referred to it as believing in the name of the Lord Jesus Christ (Acts 16:31).

Scripture says absolutely nothing about "praying a sinner's prayer," or "asking Jesus into our hearts." Jesus never requested any of these things to be done. He never promised the Spirit to those who did them. The Holy Spirit is given to those that obey the Lord, namely: believe, repent, and become baptized (Acts 2:38).

What is important is that we readily confess all that Scripture affirms about the Holy Spirit. Because of this, we can rest content, even while our minds confess and ponder the mystery of it all.

Jesus provided valuable insight (John chapters 14-16). He said that:

- the Spirit proceeded from the Father (15:26).
- the Father (God) would send the Spirit (14:26).
- He (Jesus) would send the Spirit (15:26).
- the Father would send the Spirit at Jesus' request (14:16-17).
- the Father would send the Spirit in His (Jesus') name (14:26).
- the Spirit would abide with the disciples forever (14:16-17).
- the Spirit would abide in the disciples (14:17).
- the Spirit was to be a Comforter, Counselor or Helper (14:26). The original term literally meant "one called alongside." It was also translated as "advocate" (1 John 2:1).
- the Spirit would teach the disciples all things (14:26).
- the Spirit would bring to the disciples' remembrance all things that Jesus had said (14:26).
- the Spirit would not initiate a message but would teach what He had heard (16:13).

- the Spirit came not to be an innovator, originator or imitator—the Holy Spirit's role was to call attention to Christ (16:13-15).
- the Spirit would bear witness of Jesus (15:26).
- the Spirit would glorify Jesus (16:14).

Q *How can you tell when you have the Holy Spirit? Is speaking in "tongues" the inherent evidence of having the Holy Spirit?*

A First, God promises the Holy Spirit to those who repent and are baptized, *"Peter said to them, 'Repent, and each of you be baptized in the name of Jesus Christ for the forgiveness of your sins; and you will receive the gift of the Holy Spirit'"* (Acts 2:38).

Second, God declared that He had given the Holy Spirit to those who had obeyed (repented and become baptized) Him, *"And we are witnesses of these things; and so is the Holy Spirit, whom God has given to those who obey Him"* (Acts 5:32).

Therefore, we must trust God. We must trust the promise of God that He gives the Holy Spirit when we meet the conditions. Now for those who have been given the Holy Spirit, allow Him to influence, control and dominate every dimension of your life, *"And do not get drunk with wine, for that is dissipation, but be filled with the Spirit"* (Ephesians 5:18).

One way we recognize the Holy Spirit's work in our lives is by the production of traits or behavior which are foreign to our natural selves such as love, joy, peace, patience, kindness, goodness, faithfulness, gentleness and self-control (Galatians 5:22-23).

The Bible nowhere states that being filled with the Holy Spirit is evidenced by speaking in tongues. The Bible admonishes us to be filled with the Spirit (Ephesians 5:18). When one is filled, he will relate appropriately to the Lord (Ephesians 5:21), spouse (Ephesians 5:22-33), parents (Ephesians 6:1-3), children (Ephesians 6:4).

Q Where in the Bible does it say that the Father, Son and Holy Spirit are one?

A 1 John 5:7 of the KJV says, *"For there are three that bear record in heaven, the Father, the Word, and the Holy Ghost: and these three are one."* The term trinity is never used in Scripture. However Scripture does refer to the Father, Son and Holy Spirit (Matthew 3:16-17; 28:18-19).

Q Is the Holy Ghost the same as the Holy Spirit? If so, why the distinction?

A Yes, this reference is just the translator's choice of terminology.

Q **What function does the Holy Spirit play in the life of a Christian today?**

A The Holy Spirit was given to be a helper (comforter), *"I will ask the Father, and He will give you another Helper, that He may be with you forever; that is the Spirit of truth, whom the world cannot receive, because it does not see Him or know Him, but you know Him because He abides with you and will be in you."* (John 14:16-17).

Therefore the Holy Spirit enables and energizes believers to behave consistently with the will of God. *"For this reason I bow my knees before the Father, from whom every family in heaven and on earth derives its name, that He would grant you, according to the riches of His glory, to be strengthened with power through His Spirit in the inner man, so that Christ may dwell in your hearts through faith; and that you, being rooted and grounded in love, may be able to comprehend with all the saints what is the breadth and length and height and depth, and to know the love of Christ which surpasses knowledge, that you may be filled up to all the fullness of God. Now to Him who is able to do far more abundantly beyond all that we ask or think, according to the power that works within us, to Him be the glory in the church and in Christ Jesus to all generations forever and ever. Amen"* (Ephesians (3:14-18).

Q *Does a believer have to tarry for the Holy Spirit?*

A No! Eleven of the twelve original apostles were told to wait for the Holy Spirit (Acts 1:1-4). This was done because the Holy Spirit had not yet come to dwell within human beings as He would dwell in them (John 7:37-39, 16:7). Now the Holy Spirit is given immediately to those who obey the Lord (Acts 2:38, 5:32).

Q *Explain the Holy Spirit and the gift of the Holy Spirit.*

A The **apostolic** gift—a unique and unequaled gift of the Holy Spirit to the Apostles only. Their gift of the Spirit was unique and unequaled; therefore, their power and prerogatives extended beyond that of other disciples. Every disciple was not an apostle and did not speak in tongues (1 Corinthians 12:28-30). The Holy Spirit enabled the apostles:

(1) to perform signs that only the apostles could perform (2 Corinthians 12:12).

(2) to distinguish themselves from false apostles (Revelation 2:2).

(3) to lay their hands upon other disciples and empower them to perform miracles (Acts 8:18).

The **assisting** gift—a utilitarian gift of the Spirit. It was utilitarian in that it equipped disciples to perform specific needed functions. God gave it to help in the performing of some specific thing needed at the time. (1 Corinthians 12:4-11).

This gift was neither a sign of nor a reward for advanced spiritual attainment. The disciples at Corinth possessed this gift; yet, they exhibited evidence of very low spiritual advancement (1 Corinthians 3:1-3).

It provided information, confirmation, and administration. We now have access to all of the written New Testament documents; therefore, we can validate our information, confirmation and principles of administration with principles from Scripture (2 Timothy 3:16-17; Ephesians 3:1-6).

The **abiding** gift—a universal gift of the Spirit. It was universal in that it was promised to all and was provided for all who obeyed the Lord (Acts 2:38-39, 5:32). This indwelling presence of the Holy Spirit bears witness with our spirit that we indeed are children of God (Romans 8:16, 1 Corinthians 3:16, Galatians 4:4-6).

This gift of God works with the power of the Word. God dwells in us (2 Corinthians 6:16, 1 John 4:12-16). Christ dwells in us (Romans 8:9-10; Ephesians 3:17).

The abiding gift of the Spirit is forever with the disciples; for He seals us (Ephesians 1:13, energizes us Ephesians 3:16-20 and fills us Ephesians 5:18).

Q *Why is it a sin to blaspheme against Holy Spirit, but not a sin to blaspheme against Christ (Matthew 12:30-32)?*

A Blasphemy against Christ was sin. Jesus said it would be forgiven.

While Jesus was on earth, the Holy Spirit performed his deeds through Jesus (Matthew 12:28). At that time, sin was accounted against the Holy Spirit.

Now that Jesus is no longer on earth, He performs His deeds through the Holy Spirit (John 16:12-18). Since the death of Jesus, all sins are charged against Him not the Holy Spirit. Jesus is that one perfect sin offering. Therefore, no person today can possibly commit the blasphemy against the Holy Spirit.

SALVATION

Salvation is a deliverance from an old relationship to a new relationship that takes place according to an authorized process. Salvation was a military term that described an escape from a position of danger to a position of safety (Exodus 14:13, 15-16, 21-22).

In their old relationship, the Israelites served *Pharaoh* (Exodus 5:1-2); in our old relationship we served *sin* (John 8:34).

Salvation from sin is neither biological, economical nor racial, but is a scriptural issue (2 Timothy 3:15-16).

The Bible speaks of several types of salvation. The relationships delivered from and the relationships delivered to may differ, but the principles of the process of the deliverance remain the same.

For the Israelites, God provided salvation from Pharaoh (Exodus 14:13-22).

Hundreds of years later, the apostle Paul called the culminating stage of their deliverance a baptism (1 Corinthians 10:1-2). God provided salvation for us and the apostle Peter says that it culminates with baptism (1 Peter 3:21).

Q Once we are saved are we always saved?

A Yes, if we live a life of faith, *"Blessed be the God and Father of our Lord Jesus Christ, who according to His great mercy has caused us to be born-again to a living hope through the resurrection of Jesus Christ from the dead, to obtain an inheritance which is imperishable and undefiled and will not fade away, reserved in heaven for you, who are protected by the power of God through faith for a salvation ready to be revealed in the last time"* (1 Peter 1:3-5).

No, if we abandon faith in God, *"For if, after they have escaped the defilements of the world by the knowledge of the Lord and Savior Jesus Christ, they are again entangled in them and are overcome, the last state has become worse for them than the first. For it would be better for them not to have known the way of righteousness, than having known it, to turn away from the holy commandment handed on to them. It has happened to them according to the true proverb, A dog returns to its own vomit, and, A sow, after washing, returns to wallowing in the mire"* (2 Peter 2:20-22).

When we are forgiven of sin, we become heirs of salvation. If we violate the terms of our inheritance, we can be disinherited (Hebrews 6:1-6; 2 Peter 2:20-22).

Q *How does one become a member of the Lord's organism?*

A **Believing** that Jesus is the Christ the Son of God is an adequate response of faith (John 8:24).

Repenting of sin is an adequate response of faith (Acts 17:30). Repentance is a change of mind that takes place in our heart. We must change our minds about sin. In repentance, we accepted what we had neglected and/or rejected relative to God's standard.

Becoming baptized is an adequate response of faith for it is our response to the call of God (Matthew 28:18-20; Mark 16:15-16; Acts 2:36-38; 1 Peter 3:21).

Baptism takes place while a penitent believer is in the water (Acts 8:36-39). When we believed, repented and became baptized we became forgiven, saved and a member of the church.

Those in the church are redeemed by the blood of Christ and are born-again into a state of innocence and holiness (1 Peter 1:13-23). Yet, the church consists not of imperfect, but rather purified people. One is born-again and purified by obeying the truth (1 Peter 1:22). This could only happen to those who had been taught the truth (Romans 6:17; John 6:44-45).

The church consists not of perfect people, but people who have responded favorably to the gospel of Christ. They have been born-again into the family of God.

You can be born-again, become a Christian and a relative in the family of God without ever being a part of any denomination. Becoming a part of a denomination does nothing to put one into the church of Christ.

Q *Must I do more than just believe that Jesus is the Son of God to be saved?*

A Jesus said repent and be baptized (Mark 16:16). The apostles preached repentance and baptism for the forgiveness of sin—the equivalent of being saved (Acts 2:36-38, 40-41).

Q *My son died of cancer. Will he be saved? Will he make it to heaven? Did he have a chance to make a death-bed repentance?*

A Only God Almighty knows. Only He is the judge. God has informed us to believe the gospel, repent of sin, and become baptized for the forgiveness of sin (Acts 2:37-38). He has not informed us of any exceptions. You cannot know now. Therefore, you should not even think to know now. It is human to desire to know where loved ones are. But it is not spiritual to desire to know. God never equipped us to know. Stop yearning to do what God never wanted nor equipped you to do. Just, make sure of your salvation.

Q ***If parents and grandparents are saved, will the other family members be saved by their grace?***

A We are saved by the grace of God, not relatives. God saves individuals for their individual receptiveness to Him, not on the basis of their relatives reception of Him (Acts 2:38; 47, 1 Corinthians 5:10).

Q ***Please explain Philippians 2:12, which tells us to "work out your own salvation with fear and trembling."***

A To "work out" or "work" is to bring to fruition that which is already inherently within. For example, the Scripture says, "tribulation works patience" (Romans 5:3). Patience is the flower inside the bud of tribulation. The Scripture also says that sin works death (Romans 7:13). Death is the resulting fruit of sin (Romans 7:13).

The thing "worked," though originally invisible, was already there, so that given full process it finally came into view. Salvation is bound up in our relationship with Christ, and our obedient lives are the process by which that salvation blossoms from bud to bright flower.

God further revealed, *"for it is God who is at work in you"* (Philippians 2:13). We can only "work out" what God "works in." Because we realize that God is at work in us, we live our lives obediently before God "with fear and trembling" reverential respect (2 Corinthians 7:15; Ephesians 6:5).

Church

The Scripture uses synonymously the terms "church" and "body" (Ephesians 1:22-23; Colossians 1:18). Therefore, whatever we can say truthfully about the body we can also say truthfully about the church. The Holy Spirit revealed that Jesus will ultimately save the church (Ephesians 5:23-24, 32). For this, we should have a great appreciation for the church.

The church includes all of God's people, for it is God's "new" society of people. God intends for all of His people to be one. Jesus prayed for all believers to be one, *"I do not ask on behalf of these alone, but for those also who believe in Me through their word; that they may all be one; even as You, Father, are in Me and I in You, that they also may be in Us, so that the world may believe that You sent Me"* (John 17:20-21).

There is only one church, *"And He put all things in subjection under His feet, and gave Him as head over all things to the church, which is His body, the fullness of Him who fills all in all"* (Ephesians 1:22-23). *"There is one body and one Spirit, just as also you were called in one hope of your calling"* (Ephesians 4:4).

The church of Christ is not a denomination. It is neither Baptist, Catholic, Lutheran, etc. It is not a combination of denominations. The word *denomination* suggests division. Jesus and the Holy Spirit emphasized the oneness of God's people (John 17:20-21; 1 Corinthians 12:12-13). Therefore, the very concept of a denomination for the people of God is unacceptable with Him.

Only through being born-again and being added by the Lord can one become a member of the church of Christ. Affiliation with a religious group never qualifies one to become a member of the church of Christ. God wants us to be faithful members of the church of Christ.

The church of Christ is the family of God (Ephesians 3:15). Family denotes relationship. If then the church is a family, then those within the church share a relationship with God. God is father and we are His children. The children of God share a relationship with each other. They are brothers and sisters in Christ. Yes, those within the church are spiritual relatives, related by the blood of Jesus.

Those in the church are redeemed by the blood of Christ and are born-again into a state of holiness (1 Peter 1:13-23). Yet, the church consists of imperfect, but purified, people. One is born-again and purified by obeying the truth (1 Peter 1:22). This could only happen to those who had been taught the truth (Romans 6:17; John 6:44-45).

The church consists not of perfect people, but people who have responded favorably to the gospel of Christ and have been saved from the past penalty of sin. Many links in the chain of salvation inherently connect to the church (Ephesians 5:23-33). For example:

- God is our Savior (1 Timothy 4:10; Romans 6:23).
- Jesus Christ saves (Matthew 1:21; Hebrews 5:8-9).
- The Holy Spirit saves (1 Corinthians 6:11).
- We are saved by grace (Ephesians 2:8-9).
- We are saved by the blood of Jesus (Romans 5:8-9).
- We are saved by hope (Romans 8:24).

In spite of the diversity of the members within the church, the body of Christ is one (1 Corinthians 12:12-13). Each disciple of Christ is interdependent of other disciples (1 Corinthians 12:21-26). The eye is hampered in functioning if it assumes that the hand is unnecessary. It may spot the food but cannot pick it up (1 Corinthians 12:21).

In this spiritual web of relationships, a support group emerges which ought to care for the weak, the less honorable, and the unseemly (1 Corinthians

12:26). The Christian life is relationships with others—not an isolated experience.

For spiritual growth and development, disciples should participate within a local congregation (Acts 2:41-42; 20:7; 1 Corinthians 16:1-2; 2 Thessalonians 3:6-15).

Q What is the church of Christ? Where did it come?

A The church is the organism of Jesus that He Himself promised to build (Matthew 16:13-18). Let's describe the church from the Book of Ephesians: 1:22-23, the body of Christ or church of Christ; 2:12-16, the organism unto where the forgiven are reconciled; 3:10, displays for heaven the wisdom of God; 4:4, one body or one church; 4:12, what the saints are to build up; 5:23, the organism that Christ is Head and Savior of; 5:24, the organism that is subject to Christ; 5:25, the organism that Christ loves and gave Himself for; 5:26, the organism that He will sanctify and cleanse through the teachings of His Word; 5:27, the organism that He will present to Himself; 5:29, the organism that Christ cherishes; 5:30, the organism of which the saved are members.

The Old Testament prophets predicted that God would provide a "new" institution of His people (Isaiah 2:2-3, Micah 4:1-2 and Zechariah 1:16).

That new institution would be **international** (Revelation 5:8-9).

That new institution would also be **interracial** (Galatians 3:27-29).

That new institution would also be **indestructible** (Matthew 16:18).

Unity would exist within that new institution for it would include all of God's people (John 17:20-21).

Q *What about a church home? What difference does it make what church you go to or what denomination you are a part of if you believe God?*

A Those who truly honor God according to His Word will do some things and refuse to do some other things. God has always wanted his people to be an organized community of believers. To have community you must have policy and procedure. God made a covenant with Moses and gave him the Ten Commandments.

Even now, God wants His people to be accountable to one another within a body of believers.

"Be on guard for yourselves and for all the flock, among which the Holy Spirit has made you overseers, to shepherd the church of God which He purchased with His own blood" (Acts 20:28). *"and be subject to one another in the fear of Christ"* (Ephesians 5:21).

We must avoid those who refuse to teach truth, *"Now I urge you, brethren, keep your eye on those who cause dissensions and hindrances contrary to the teaching which you learned, and turn away from them"* (Romans 16:17).

"Anyone who goes too far and does not abide in the teaching of Christ, does not have God; the one who abides in the teaching, he has both the Father and the Son. If anyone comes to you and does not bring this teaching, do not receive him into your house, and do not give him a greeting; for the one who gives him a greeting participates in his evil deeds" (2 John 1:9-11).

Q What is worship?
A Worship is our expression to glorify God. Our expressions of worship must be compatible with the nature of God.

Worship is our expression of allegiance to God (Genesis 22:1-14, John 4:20-24). Worship is our expression of appreciation to God (Exodus 14:30-15:21, Matthew 1:18-2:11).

Worship is our expression to benefit one another. Our expressions must be compatible with the needs of one another.

Worship is for human edification (1 Corinthians 14:13-15, 1 Corinthians 14:11-31).

Worship is for human motivation (Acts 4:23-31, 16 25-40). It motivates us and those who hear (Acts 4:23-31, 4:32-35, 16:25-40). Worship should be a matter of spiritual conviction.

Q By whose authority are we commanded to meet and worship on the first day of the week?

A God has always authorized His people to worship on the first day of the week (Exodus 12:16, Leviticus 23:2-3, 7-8, 21, 24, 27, 35-37; Numbers 28:18, 25-26; Numbers 29:1, 7).

Q *Is the church that Jesus is coming back for the 144,000?*

A Nothing within Scripture suggests that. In the vision of the apostle John, he saw 144,000 (12,000 from each of the twelve tribes) on earth. *"After this I saw four angels standing at the four corners of the earth, holding back the four winds of the earth, so that no wind would blow on the earth or on the sea or on any tree. And I saw another angel ascending from the rising of the sun, having the seal of the living God; and he cried out with a loud voice to the four angels to whom it was granted to harm the earth and the sea, saying, Do not harm the earth or the sea or the trees until we have sealed the bond-servants of our God on their foreheads. And I heard the number of those who were sealed, one hundred and forty-four thousand sealed from every tribe of the sons of Israel: the tribe of Judah, twelve thousand were sealed, from the tribe of Reuben twelve thousand, from the tribe of Gad twelve thousand, the tribe of Asher twelve thousand, from the tribe of Naphtali twelve thousand, from the tribe of Manasseh twelve thousand, the tribe of Simeon twelve thousand, from the tribe of Levi twelve thousand, from the tribe of Issachar twelve thousand, the tribe of Zebulun twelve thousand, from the tribe of Joseph twelve thousand, from the tribe of Benjamin, twelve thousand were sealed"* (Revelation 7:1-8).

Also within his vision, the Apostle John saw an innumerable number in heaven, *"After these things I looked, and behold, a great multitude which no one could count, from every nation and all tribes and peoples and tongues, standing before the throne and before the Lamb, clothed in white robes, and palm branches were in their hands; and they cry out with a loud voice, saying, Salvation to our God who sits on the throne, and to the Lamb"* (Revelation 7:9).

SABBATH

The Hebrews celebrated a *holy convocation* on the *first and the seventh day* of the Passover feast. (Exodus 12:16). Again, they celebrated a *holy convocation on the first, seventh, and eighth, tenth and fifteenth* day (Leviticus 23:2-3, 7-8, 21-27, 35-37, Numbers 28:18-26).

Within scripture, there is no mention of any type of holy convocation for the Sabbath that was not celebrated on other days as well. Jesus taught daily as well as on the Sabbath (Luke 19:47; 22:53). He elevated mercy above sacrifice or Sabbath observance (Matthew 12:1-13; Mark 3:1-7; Luke 6:1-11).

God's covenant with Jesus Christ emphasizes Sunday, the first day of the week, as a day for Christians worship. Let's observe some unique occurrences that took place on Sunday, the first day of the week.

- On Sunday, Jesus named His apostles (Luke 6:1-16).
- On Sunday, Jesus rose from the dead (Luke 24:1-8).
- On Sunday, Jesus met with His disciples after His resurrection for the first time (John 20:19-20).
- On Sunday, prophecy was fulfilled as the Holy Spirit fell on the apostles (Joel 2:28-32; Acts 2:1-21; John 16:13).
- On Sunday, Jesus was preached as both Christ and Lord for the first time (Acts 2:36).
- On Sunday, baptism for the forgiveness for sins was performed by the apostles for the first time (Luke 24:46-47; Acts 2:36-38).
- On Sunday, disciples contributed of their financial resources (1 Corinthians 16:1-2).
- On Sunday, disciples observed the Lord's Supper (Acts 20:7).

Q *When did the Sabbath day become significant? What is significant about the Sabbath day?*

A In six days God created the world, but on the seventh day, He rested (Genesis 2:1-2). After resting on the seventh day, God sanctified it (Genesis 2:3). God blessed and sanctified the seventh day because He (had) rested (Genesis 2:1-3). It seems that He blessed it after He had rested. We have a Biblical record of God giving laws to humankind on the 6th day (Genesis 1:28), but we have no Biblical record of God giving the Sabbath law to humankind on the 6th nor the 7th day.

It was the seventh day of the week, a day of rest (Genesis 2:2-3). In addition to the weekly Sabbath, there was a yearly Sabbath (Exodus 23:10-13; (Leviticus 25:1-7). Initially, the Sabbath was a day of rest for God (Hebrews 4:4). Scripture said absolutely nothing about human beings being commanded to observe the Sabbath until centuries after the creation (Exodus 16:22-30; 20:9-13). The Sabbath rest was a sign of the covenant between God and the Israelites whom He delivered from Egypt (Exodus 31:12-18; Ezekiel 20:8-11).

Q How was the Sabbath day to be kept?

A Resting satisfied the total demand of the Sabbath (Jeremiah 17:21-27; Nehemiah 13:16-22; Exodus 20:8-11; 31:12-17). People of the New Testament understood the Sabbath to be a day of rest (Luke 23:56). However, the Sabbath did become a day for Jewish worship (Ezekiel 46:3).

Q What was the penalty for violating the Sabbath?

A Those who had the Sabbath command of rest also had the command to stone to death those who violated it (Exodus 35:1-2). Picking up sticks defiled the Sabbath (Numbers 15:32;

Nehemiah 13:16-22; Jeremiah 17:21-27). And they did stone to death those who worked on the Sabbath (Numbers 15:32-36).

Q *What behavior was prohibited on the Sabbath?*
A Some of the Sabbath prohibitions included: going out and picking up food (Exodus 16:29), allowing children, servants and/or animals to work (Exodus 20:8-11), kindling fire (Exodus 35:2-3), picking up sticks (Numbers 15:32), buying and selling (Nehemiah 13:15-22).

Q *Did Jesus observe the Sabbath?*
A Yes. Jesus kept the Passover and every other Jewish feast day (Matthew 26:17-18). He also kept all the Law of Moses, including the offering of animal sacrifices (Luke 5:14).

Q *When was the Sabbath first observed by humankind?*
A God commanded human beings to observe the Sabbath for the first time after they had left Egypt (Exodus 16:22-30).

Q *For the first Sabbath observance, did the people of God worship or cease from work?*
A The first Sabbath observance was for rest, not worship (Exodus 16:22-30).

Q *Is Sunday the Christian Sabbath? If so, do we sin when work on Sunday?*

A Sunday is not the Sabbath. The word Sabbath had a dual meaning—7th and rest (Genesis 2:2-3). It was the seventh day of the week. Sunday as we know it, is the first day of the week. The Sabbath was the seventh day of the week. Therefore, the Sabbath was the day before the first day of the week, Sunday (Matthew 28:1).

Initially only God rested. The first Biblical record of human beings observing a Sabbath rest was hundreds of years after the creation (Exodus 16:22-30).

This command to rest was given only to the Israelites (Exodus 20:1-11). Those who had the Sabbath command of rest also had the command to stone to death those who violated it (Exodus 35:1-2). And they did stone to death those who worked on the Sabbath (Numbers 15:32-36).

Q *What is the difference between the Law of God and the Law of Moses?*

A **The Law of God is the Law of Moses.** Let's observe the interchangeableness of the different designations of the law.

Nehemiah 8:1-8:

(vs. 1) "Law of Moses"

(vs. 3) "Book of the Law"

(vs. 8) "Law of God"

(vs. 14) "Law which God commanded by Moses"

(vs. 18) "Law of God"

Nehemiah 10:29—Moses gave the Law of God.

Ezra 7:6-21—The Law of Moses is equivalent to the Law of God

(vs. 6) "Scribe of the Law of Moses"

(vs. 10) "Law of the Lord"

(vs. 12) "Law of the God of heaven"

(vs. 21) "Scribe of the Law of God

Deuteronomy 5:1-21 the covenant made at Horeb contained the Ten Commandments.

Malachi 4:4 the covenant made at Horeb was called the Law of Moses; therefore, the Law of Moses contained the Ten Commandments.

Matthew 15:4 Jesus made no difference between what God and what Moses had said. Mark 7:10

Resting satisfied the demand of the Sabbath. Resting satisfied the total demand of the Sabbath (Jeremiah 17:21-27; Nehemiah 13:16-22; Exodus 20:8-11; 31:12-17). People of the New Testament understood the Sabbath to be a day of rest (Luke 23:56). However, the Sabbath did become a day for Jewish worship (Ezekiel 46:3).

Those who had the Sabbath command of rest also had the command to stone to death those who violated it (Exodus 35:1-2). Picking up sticks defiled the Sabbath (Numbers 15:32; Nehemiah 13:16-22; Jeremiah 17:21-27). And they did stone to death those who worked on the Sabbath (Numbers 15:32-36).

Genesis 2:1-3—God rested on the 7th day. **Resting** created and sanctioned the Sabbath as a holy day. In six days God created the world, but on the seventh day He rested (Genesis 2:1-2). After resting on the seventh day, God sanctified it (Genesis 2:3). God blessed and sanctified the seventh day because He (had) rested (Genesis 2:1-3). It seems that He blessed it after He had rested. We have a Biblical record of God giving laws to humankind on the 6th day (Genesis 1:28), but we have no Biblical record of God giving the Sabbath law to humankind on the 6th nor the 7th day.

Exodus 16:23-30—Thousands of years after God **rested**, we have the first mention within Scripture of any specific directives for human being to observe the Sabbath. **Resting** satisfied totally the requirement for a holy Sabbath. The covenant that God made with the Israelites at Sinai (Horeb) was not made with those of the previous generation (Deuteronomy 5:1-3).

Exodus 20:8-11 Within the **first** listing of the **Ten Commandments**, *resting* satisfied totally the requirement for a holy Sabbath (Deuteronomy 5:12-15).

Exodus 23:12—**Resting** satisfied totally the requirement for a holy Sabbath.

Exodus 31:15-17—**Resting** satisfied totally the requirement for a holy Sabbath.

Exodus 34:21—**Resting** satisfied totally the requirement for a holy Sabbath.

Exodus 35:1-3—**Resting** satisfied totally the requirement for a holy Sabbath.

Leviticus 23:3—**Resting** satisfied totally the requirement for a holy Sabbath. It satisfied **totally** the requirement for a **holy convocation**.

Numbers 15:32-36—Refusing to **rest** profaned the Sabbath.

Luke 23:56—**Resting** satisfied totally the requirement for a holy Sabbath.

Exodus 12:16—The Hebrews celebrated a **holy convocation** on the **first and the seventh day** of the Passover feast.

Leviticus 23:2-3, 7-8—The Hebrews celebrated a **holy convocation** on the **first, seventh, and** 21, 24, 27, 35-37 **eighth day.**

Numbers 28:18—The Hebrews celebrated a **holy convocation** on the **first** and **seventh** 25-26 **day.**

Numbers 29:1, 7 The Hebrews celebrated a **holy convocation on** the **first, tenth** and 12, 35 **fifteenth day.**

Within Scripture, there is no mention of any type of holy convocation for the Sabbath that was not celebrated on other days as well. Jesus taught daily as well as on the Sabbath (Luke 19:47; 22:53). He elevated mercy above sacrifice or Sabbath observance (Matthew 12:1-13; Mark 3:1-7; Luke 6:1-11).

Some of the Sabbath prohibitions included:

(1) Exodus 16:29—going out and picking up food

(2) Exodus 20:8-11—allowing children, servants and/or animals to work.

(3) Exodus 35:2-3—kindling fire

(4) Numbers 15:32—picking up sticks

(5) Nehemiah 13:15-22—buying and selling

Jesus kept the Passover and every other Jewish feast day (Matthew 26:17-18). He also kept all the Law of Moses including the offering of animal sacrifices (Luke 5:14). Those who subscribe to the Sabbath need to say why they don't follow Jesus' example. Was there ever a law that God gave relaxing any of the Sabbath day restrictions? No!

We do have references of the apostle Paul preaching on the Sabbath day to non-Christian Jews, those who were lost without Jesus. Should this surprise us?

Just because the very first preaching of the Gospel occurred on the day of Pentecost, it does not mean Christians must keep Pentecost (Acts 2:1-38). Paul also rushed to get back to Jerusalem on Pentecost (Acts 20:16). Pentecost always fell on a Sunday. Does this mean he was keeping a Pentecost feast? No. It provided him a great opportunity to teach those who had assembled.

Questions that must be answered:

(1) Is Exodus 16:22-30 the first mention of a Sabbath ordinance for man? On this first occasion, did God command rest? On this first occasion, did He command worship?
(2) Which feast should we continue to observe, Passover, Pentecost or Tabernacles?
(3) How does one defile the Sabbath today?

(4) Who, when and why was the death penalty removed for defiling the Sabbath? (Numbers 15:32-36).
(5) Did selling and buying profane the Sabbath (Nehemiah 13:16-22)? Does selling and buying profane the Sabbath now?
(6) Do we now have a better ministry (Hebrews 8:6)?
(7) Do we need to keep a year long Sabbath every seven years? Why? Why not (Leviticus 25:1-4; 12)? Who, when, and why was it removed?

Christianity was not a mere continuation of Judaism, "Behold, days are coming, declares the Lord, when I will make a new covenant with the house of Israel, and with the house of Judah, not like the covenant which I made with their fathers in the day that I took them by the hand to bring them out of the land of Egypt..." (Jeremiah 31:31-32). God said He would make a "new" covenant that would not be like the covenant that he made with their fathers when He brought them out of the land of Egypt.

Which covenant did God make with Israel when He led them out of Egypt? "There was nothing in the ark except the two tablets of stone which Moses put there at Horeb, where the Lord made a covenant with the sons of Israel, when they came out of the land of Egypt" (1 Kings 8:9). These two tablets of stone refer to the Ten Commandments. But this was the covenant which was made when they came out of the land of Egypt. According to Jeremiah the new covenant would not be like this one. Hebrews 8:7-13 clearly shows that Jeremiah 31:31-32 has been fulfilled.

The Ten Commandment law, including the requirement to keep the Sabbath Day, was abolished at the cross along with all the rest of the Law of Moses. God gave a covenant at Mt. Sinai through Moses to the Jews. No one prior to Moses (Abraham or Adam) ever heard of the Sabbath law, much less kept it.

Jesus said, "Do not think that I came to abolish the Law, or the Prophets; I did not come to abolish, but to fulfill" (Matthew 5:17). The key to understanding verse 17 is found in verse 18: "For truly I say to you, until heaven and earth pass away, not the smallest letter or stroke shall pass from the Law, until all is accomplished." The Law would not pass "until all is accomplished." Until means that the Law of Moses would last "up until" the time that all of it was accomplished (fulfilled).

The apostle Paul discussed the Law of Moses being nailed to the cross (Colossians 2:14). Again, he obviously spoke of the Law that included the Ten Commandments, not just the penalty or some ceremonial portion (Romans 7:6-13).

The Mosaic Dispensation (Old Testament) does not govern us, but the Christian Dispensation (New Testament) does. Let us examine the transition from the Mosaic to the Christian Dispensation, 16) "Now the promises were spoken to Abraham and to his seed. He does not say, "And to seeds," as referring to many, but rather to one, "And to your seed," that is, Christ…19) Why the Law then? It was added because of transgressions, having been ordained through angels by the agency of a mediator, until the seed would come to whom the promise had been made… 24) Therefore the Law has become our tutor to lead us to Christ, so that we may be justified by faith. 25) But now that faith has come, we are no longer under a tutor. 26) For you are all sons of God through faith in Christ Jesus. 27) For all of you who were baptized into Christ have clothed yourselves with Christ" (Galatians 3:16-19).

The Law had not always been in effect. God had governed humankind without the Law of Moses. He governed Moses for over 80 years without the Law; for Moses was over 80 years old when God revealed the Law to him at Mt. Sinai (Exodus 7:7; Acts 7:23-30).

God added the Law because of the waywardness of humankind. By attaching penalties to sin, the Law increased awareness of sin. Even the Ten Commandments ordered punishment for its violators (Exodus 35:1-3; Numbers 15:32-36). How many people would drive the speed limit if there was no penalty (fine) for speeding? Penalties increase our awareness of violations of the law.

The Law was designed to last until the seed should come (Galatians 3:19). Jesus Christ was that seed (Galatians 3:16). The Law was designed to last until Jesus came into the world. It brought us to Christ and then Christ released us from the Law (Galatians 3:24-25). We are children of God by faith in Jesus Christ, not by the Law of Moses (Galatians 3:26-27).

Q *On what day did Jesus customarily worship? Does Luke 4:16 "And He came to Nazareth, where He had been brought up; and as was His custom, He entered the synagogue on the Sabbath, and stood up to read" prove that the Sabbath is still the day for us to worship?*

A It is true that the text of Luke 4:16 teaches that Jesus had a custom of doing something on the Sabbath. But what did he do?

Jesus went into the synagogue, and stood up to read. Should we equate standing up to read as being worship?

Let's proceed as if this is indeed worship. According to Luke, Jesus taught in the temple every day "And He was teaching daily in the temple; but the chief priests and the scribes and the leading men among the people were trying to destroy Him" (Luke 19:47). *"While I was with you daily in the temple, you did not lay hands on Me; but this hour and the power of darkness are yours"* (Luke 22:53).

Luke mentions only once that Jesus taught in the synagogue on the Sabbath, but he mentions **twice** that Jesus taught every day. Within Scripture, more is said about Jesus teaching every day than just on the Sabbath. Obviously then, Jesus had a custom of worshiping every day.

The apostles, under the direct guidance of the Holy Spirit, taught every day, not just on the Sabbath "Day by day continuing with one mind in the temple, and breaking bread from house to house, they were taking their meals together with gladness and sincerity of heart, praising God and having favor with all the people. And the Lord was adding to their number day by day those who were being saved." (Acts 2:46-47); "And every day, in the temple and from house to house, they kept right on teaching and preaching Jesus as the Christ" (Acts 5:42).

"Now these were more noble-minded than those in Thessalonica, for they received the word with great eagerness, examining the Scriptures daily to see whether these things were so." (Acts 17:11). The apostle Paul commended these disciples for their daily worship (Acts 17:11).

It is very misleading to advance the idea that Luke 4:16 elevate Sabbath worship above worship on any other day of the week.

PRAYER

Prayer is a verbalization or speaking of our faith. Jesus taught His disciples to "say" something when they prayed (Luke 11:2). Faith is what we do about what we believe that indeed the Lord has said (2 Corinthians 4:13). What we say reinforces what we believe.

But prayer is not just what we say. Prayer is that which we say, that we have seen through faith. Before we can say something, we must first see it. When someone asks for directions to your house, first you visualize traveling the streets that lead to your house. Only after you visualize can you then say what they are. Mental pictures precede verbal pronouncements. We may not always be able to say what we see, but we can never say what we cannot see.

Prayer is a visualization of our faith. God wanted His people to visualize prayer. The rising incense visibly symbolized the prayers of the saints rising toward God *"When He had taken the book, the four living creatures and the twenty-four elders fell down before the Lamb, each one holding a harp and golden bowls full of incense, which are the prayers of the saints"* (Revelation 5:8). *"Another angel came and stood at the altar, holding a golden censer; and much incense was given to him, so that he might add it to the prayers of all the saints on the golden altar which was before the throne. And the smoke of the incense, with the prayers of the saints, went up before God out of the angel's hand"* (Revelation 8:3-4).

Prayer is a seeing of our faith in God. We see God listening and waiting to respond to our prayer. It is very difficult to ask a favor of someone whom we believe is not listening to respond. When we do not believe that God is listening, we pray hesitantly and timidly. Seeing a God who listens to respond encourages us to pray boldly.

Q *How do I pray correctly?*
A Find a prayer that was answered or one prayed for by a Holy Spirit filled person and model after that (Matthew 6, Luke 11).

Q *Must I be on my knees when I pray?*
A No. When Jesus gave his disciples the model prayer, He made no mention of any particular

physical posture (Luke 11:1-4). On one occasion Jesus knelt and prayed (Luke 22:41), while on another occasion He fell on His face and prayed (Matthew 26:39).

Q *If God is in control, should we make specific requests of Him? Is it arrogant of us to suggest to the Creator what He should do?*

A We pray because God invites us to pray. If He did not invite us, we should not dare to do it. But He takes note of us, and He invites us to come to Him, bringing our praise and thanksgiving, our confession of sins, our supplications for others, our own perceived needs—in short, with all our requests great and small. *So "let us therefore draw near with confidence to the throne of grace, that we may receive mercy and may find grace to help in time of need"* (Hebrews. 4:16).

When we bring our requests to God, we express our dependence on Him, our need of Him, our gratitude to Him and our love for him. Hopefully, we also present ourselves to Him for His service—sometimes we participate in God's answer to our own prayers! Certainly we do not "suggest what he should do" in any presumptuous way. God does not need anyone's counsel (Isaiah 40:13-14; Romans 11:34). God might say "No" to some of our requests sometimes because our motives are selfish (James 4:3).

Q *How do you determine when the Lord answers and how do you interpret?*

A God always answers. Therefore, pray and accept the results.

(1) God gives exactly what we request (Luke 1:13).

(2) God gives less than we request (Deuteronomy 1:34-46, 3:23-27, 32:50-52, Numbers 27:13, 20:12, Psalms 106:32-33).

(3) God gives other than what we request (2 Corinthians 12:7-9).

(4) God gives more than what we request (1 Kings 3:9-14; 2 Chronicles 1:10-12).

Q *Why is it important to pray daily?*

A First we must understand what prayer is. Prayer is a verbalization of our faith; *"And He said to them, When you pray "say"* (Luke 11:2). We speak to our heavenly Father about our beliefs and behaviors that are established upon scripturally valid evidences.

Also prayer is a visualization of our faith. Before you can say something, you must first see a mental picture. We see our heavenly Father listening to respond. In prayer, we exalt His name and expect His nature.

Prayer is our reaction to God's action. When we react appropriately, He then reacts favorably to our reactions. When we pray *daily*, we allow God to *daily* react favorably to us. Prayer activates the favor of God (James 4:2).

Q Can God hear the sinner's (non-Christian's) prayer?

A Yes. God hears and knows all that is thought or said. However, He has only promised to respond to the prayers of those who are in a covenant relationship with Him (1 Peter 3:12). He may respond to the prayer of a sinner, but has not covenanted to do so. Some would say what about the sinner in the temple (Luke 18:10)? This man was a Jew. Had he not been a Jew, he could not have entered the temple (Acts 21:27-28). Jews were in a covenant relationship with God. He had only sinned.

Q When you pray one thing, should you continue to pray for the same thing over an over?

A It depends. Jesus prayed for the same thing three times (Matthew 26:39, 42, 44). Repetition should not, however, indicate lack of confidence.

Q Repeat what you said about Jesus only answering prayers for the righteous.

A Read 1 Peter 3:10-12.

Q I recently converted from Catholicism to holiness. Is it wrong to pray the rosary?

A Yes. We ought to discover within Scripture our model for praying. Jesus teaches us how to pray (Luke 11:1-4). He teaches us to focus our prayer toward God for exalting His name and expecting His nurture, not the system of the rosary.

Forgiveness

God forgave His people. He then ordered His people to forgive one another (Ephesians 4:32). Forgiveness is therapeutic. Forgiveness contributes to our psychological, physiological, and soteriological well-being.

We hesitate to forgive because of the presence of false notions about the nature of forgiveness. Also, we hesitate to forgive because of the absence of true notions about the nature of forgiveness. An excellent article about forgiveness appeared in the May 1986 issue of *Reader's Digest* entitled: "Could They Forgive Their Son's Killer." I recommend reading it.

Because their father favored him, Joseph's brothers developed a revengeful hatred for him and sold him into Egyptian slavery (Genesis 37:3-4, 26-28).

Through slavery, they deprived Joseph of years with his family, but he readily forgave them Genesis 50:15-21). You can forgive those who have committed wrongs against you.

Q What does it mean to forgive?
A There are many false notions about forgiveness.

(1) Forgiveness is not forgetting. Your intellectual capacity is powerless to intentionally erase memory. *"Then Peter came and said to Him, "Lord, how often shall my brother sin against me and I forgive him? ...Jesus said to him, "I do not say to you, up to seven times, but up to seventy times seven. For this reason, the kingdom of heaven may be compared to a king who wished to settle accounts with his slaves.... Then summoning him, his lord said to him, 'You wicked slave, I forgave you all that debt because you pleaded with me."* (Matthew 18:21-35; 1 Corinthians 6:9-1). The Lord remembered who and what He had forgiven.

(2) Forgiveness is not excusing the guilty away from justice (Exodus 22:1; Leviticus 6:1-7; Numbers 5:6-7; 14:18; 2 Samuel 12:6; 9-23; Luke 19:1-10; John 5:1-14). To the woman caught in adultery Jesus said, *"...I do not condemn you, either. Go. From now on sin no more."* (John 8:11). Justice is moral accountability.

(3) Forgiveness is not necessarily restoring the relationship in every dimension as it was before. The father reserved the inheritance

posture for the older son only. To the older son the father said, "...*all that is mine is yours*" (Luke 15:31).

You may discover that the previous posture may have been unhealthy. Why restore that which is unhealthy? Forgiveness requires one changed heart. Restoration requires two changed hearts.

There needs to be true notions about forgiveness.

(1) Forgiveness is surrendering the right to retaliation, "To sum up, all of you be harmonious, sympathetic, brotherly, kindhearted, and humble in spirit; not returning evil for evil or insult for insult, but giving a blessing instead; for you were called for the very purpose that you might inherit a blessing." (1 Peter 3:8-9). Our lust for revengeful satisfaction drives our desire to see our enemy suffer.

(2) Forgiveness is a revising of our thoughtful feelings toward the guilty, "You have heard that it was said, You shall love your neighbor and hate your enemy.' But I say to you, love your enemies and pray for those who persecute you, so that you may be sons of your Father who is in heaven; for He causes His sun to rise on the evil and the good, and sends rain on the righteous and the unrighteous. For if you love those who love you, what reward do you have? Do not even the tax collectors do the same? If you greet only your brothers, what more are you doing than others. Do not even the Gentiles

do the same? Therefore you are to be perfect, as your heavenly Father is perfect" (Matthew 5:43-48). This revision expresses our nature.

(3) Forgiveness is rediscovering the humanity of the person who wronged us, *"Sufficient for such a one is this punishment which was inflicted by the majority, so that on the contrary you should rather forgive and comfort him otherwise such a one might be overwhelmed by excessive sorrow. Wherefore I urge you to reaffirm your love for him. For to this end also I wrote, so that I might put you to the test, whether you are obedient in all things. But one whom you forgive anything, I forgive also; for indeed what I have forgiven, if I have forgiven anything, I did it for your sakes in the presence of Christ, so that no advantage would be taken of us by Satan, for we are not ignorant of his schemes"* (2 Corinthians 2:6-11). We elevate them to the level of being a human being rather than reduce them to their behavior.

Q *What's the difference between repentance and forgiveness?*

A To repent is to change our mind about our own behavior. To forgive is to change our mind about the guilty status of another.

Q *How do I forgive deep hurts and heal from them?*

A Grieve your misery, *"For if I cause you sorrow, who then makes me glad but the one whom I made sorrowful? This is the very thing I wrote you, so that when I came, I would not have sorrow from those who ought to make me rejoice; having confidence in you all that my joy would be the joy of you all. For out of much affliction and anguish of heart I wrote to you with many tears; not so that you would be made sorrowful, but that you might know the love which I have especially for you."* (2 Corinthians 2:3-4).

You have suffered a great loss. In some cases, you have suffered an irretrievable loss. You have been robbed of your innocence, security, reputation, peace, joy, and family. Therefore, you have a right to grieve your misery. What you lost can seldom come back to you. You can go on with life, but before you do, you must take time to grieve.

Jacob stole his brother Esau's birthright and blessing. Esau wept loudly, *"When Esau heard the words of his father, he cried out with an exceedingly great and bitter cry, and said to his father, "Bless me, even me also, O my father!" And he said, "Your brother came deceitfully and has taken away your blessing." Then he said, "Is he not rightly named Jacob, for he has supplanted me these two times? He took away my birthright, and behold, now he has taken away my blessing." And he said, "Have you not reserved a blessing for me?" But Isaac replied* to Esau, *"Behold, I have made him your master, and all his relatives I have given to him as servants; and with grain and new wine I have sustained him. Now as for you then, what can I do, my son?" Esau said to his father, "Do you have only one blessing, my father? Bless me, even me also, O my father." So Esau lifted his voice and wept."* (Genesis 27:34-38).

But, Esau forgave his brother Jacob and proceeded with his life, *"Then Esau ran to meet him and embraced him, and fell on his neck and kissed him, and they wept.... But Esau said, "I have plenty, my brother; let what you have be your own."* (Genesis 33:4-9).

"Blessed be the God and Father of our Lord Jesus Christ, the Father of mercies and God of all comfort, who comforts us in all our affliction so that we will be able to comfort those who are in any affliction with the comfort with which we ourselves are comforted by God. For just as the sufferings of Christ are ours in abundance, so also our comfort is abundant through Christ" (2 Corinthians 1:3-5).

Place your hurt on the expressway of God's grace. Drive beyond the shock and denial of what has happened. Find a safe confidante to trust with your pain. Select someone who is ahead of you in his spiritual maturity.

The accusers broke into the room and brought this woman to Jesus. They spilled out her most recent fault (John 8:1-11). Those who are least qualified to condemn always will.

Those who are most qualified to condemn usually will not.

Choke the flames of unforgiveness. Deliberately decide to stop fanning the flames of hatred. It may help to talk to the spiritually mature, but talking just to keep the wound open is a dangerous hazard. Chose to forgive the unforgivable.

Forgiveness takes place in the mind of the one who holds the charge. God decides to forgive because of Jesus, *"...Be kind to one another, tender-hearted, forgiving each other, just as God in Christ also has forgiven you"* (Ephesians 4:32).

Forgive because God has forgiven you. If Jesus is enough to cause God to forgive you, should He not be enough to cause you to forgive others? All God requires is the blood of Jesus. Why should you require more than God does to forgive? Forgive because God has insisted upon it.

Q *How do I obtain strength to forgive those who have mistreated me when I do not think that they deserve to be forgiven?*

A Recognize the basis for forgiveness (Ephesians 4:32). We forgive others not because of them or us, but because God has forgiven us because of Jesus Christ.

After you recognize that, then forgive quickly, realizing that your unwillingness to forgive others jeopardizes your own forgiveness by God (Matthew 6:14-15).

Q *I was watching the program a few weeks ago about forgiveness. I understand that we are to forgive because God forgives us. How can you forgive if you can't trust the person? I have been betrayed more than once by my boyfriend. I need direction and guidance for me and for my boyfriend.*

A You may have confused forgiveness and restoration. Remember forgiveness does not demand restoration to the previous posture in all dimensions. The father forgave his younger son; but did not restore his inheritance privileges. He said to the older son, *"And he said to him, 'Son, you have always been with me, and all that is mine is yours"* (Luke 15:31).

While you are dating, you should be in an uncommitted posture. Extreme differences and irritations usually suggest a high degree of incompatibility. Therefore, you probably should end that relationship.

Q *How do you know that you are forgiven by God?*

A We know that we are forgiven because God has said that we are forgiven. Whom has He said are forgiven? Those who have repented and been baptized for the forgiveness of sin. Peter said to them, *"Repent, and each of you be bap-*

tized in the name of Jesus Christ for the forgiveness of your sins; and you will receive the gift of the Holy Spirit." (Acts 2:38).

Q Have you really forgiven a person if you speak kindly to them on the outside; but can't stand them on the inside?

A (1) Forgiveness is surrendering the right to retaliation. *"To sum up, all of you be harmonious, sympathetic, brotherly, kindhearted, and humble in spirit; not returning evil for evil or insult for insult, but giving a blessing instead; for you were called for the very purpose that you might inherit a blessing"* (1 Peter 3:8-9). Our lust for revengeful satisfaction drives our desire to see our enemy suffer.

(2) Forgiveness is a revising of our thoughtful feelings toward the guilty. *"You have heard that it was said, You shall love your neighbor and hate your enemy.' But I say to you, love your enemies and pray for those who persecute you, so that you may be sons of your Father who is in heaven; for He causes His sun to rise on the evil and the good, and sends rain on the righteous and the unrighteous. For if you love those who love you, what reward do you have? Do not even the tax collectors do the same? If you greet only your brothers, what more are you doing than others? Do not even the Gentiles do the same? Therefore you are to be perfect, as your heavenly Father is perfect"* (Matthew 5:43-48).

(3) Forgiveness is rediscovering the humanity of the person who wronged us. "Sufficient for such a one is this punishment which was inflicted by the majority, so that on the contrary you should rather forgive and comfort him otherwise such a one might be overwhelmed by excessive sorrow. Wherefore I urge you to reaffirm your love for him. For to this end also I wrote, so that I might put you to the test, whether you are obedient in all things. But one whom you forgive anything, I forgive also; for indeed what I have forgiven, if I have forgiven anything, I did it for your sakes in the presence of Christ, so that no advantage would be taken of us by Satan, for we are not ignorant of his schemes" (2 Corinthians 2:6-11). We elevate them to the level of being a human being rather than reduce them to their behavior.

Q When you sin and go to God for forgiveness, do you have to tell anybody else?

A No. *"If we confess our sins, He is faithful and righteous to forgive us our sins and to cleanse us from all unrighteousness"* (1 John 1:9).

The word "confess" is translated from the Greek word "homologeo" ("homo" means same, and "logeo" means to speak). Hence, confess means to speak by saying the same thing as another. It means to acknowledge, to admit, or to agree with.

First, we confess to God, for He holds the charge of guilt against us. Therefore, we must first agree with or admit to God that indeed we are guilty. When we sin, God says, "You are guilty." We must say the same thing about ourselves that God says about us. God said that we are guilty; therefore, we must also say, "Yes God, I am guilty." All sin is against God. He already knows that we are guilty. Therefore, our confession is not to reveal to God, but is an opportunity for us to agree with God, for He holds the charge of guilt against us.

Second, we confess to those who hold the charge of guilt against us. We only need to confess to those who hold a charge against us. We can inform others who are unaware, but we do not have to.

Q *Please address forgiveness in respect to African-Americans dealing with daily struggles, i.e. discrimination, racism.*

A There are two approaches to discrimination and racism. (1) Legal. Follow and exhaust the extent of legal procedure. (2) Spiritual. Forgive those for the uncorrected issues. Life is not always fair. To the extent that you can rehabilitate, do so, but do not become involved in retaliation.

SIN

Actively, we serve sin by doing that which is unauthorized by the Lord (1 John 3:4). Passively, we serve sin by refusing to do that which is authorized by the Lord (James 4:17).

We sin when our hearts oppose God. God charges us with guilt when we sin. He holds a guilty charge against us because our hearts have been opposed to Him. The guilt is of the inward person, the heart. Jesus said "*out of the heart proceed evil...*" (Matthew 15:18-19). Sin exists as an attitude long before it materializes into an action.

Guilt pains our hearts, and as a result, forgiveness of sin is a very basic need of humankind. Without the forgiveness of God, we can never become acceptable to Him, regardless of what we may humanly accomplish. Without forgiveness of sin, nothing else really matters!

Only God can cancel our charge of guilt. When God forgives He simply changes our status from guilty to not guilty.

Q What is the definition of sin?

A Active sin: *"Everyone who practices sin also practices lawlessness; and sin is lawlessness"* (1 John 3:4).

Passive sin: *"Therefore, to one who knows the right thing to do and does not do it, to him it is sin"* (James 4:17).

Q Where does sin come from?

A Sin comes from Satan (John 8:44; Genesis 3:4; Romans 5:12).

Q Are all sins equal? Are there little sins and big sins?

A Sin is sin. The intrinsic nature of all sin is equal. All sin demands the death of Jesus. However, the instrumental nature of sin may differ. For example, if you hate me without just cause the effect is different than if you murder me. Both are wrong but the instrumental effect is different.

Q *Are some sins worse than others? When Eli failed to control the sinful behavior of his sons, God cursed them (I Samuel 2:22-23; 3:11-14), but when Samuel's sons did not follow God (1 Samuel 8:3), there was no mention of the type of punishment. Are some sins more serious than others?"*

A I do not think we need to rank the various sins of Eli's sons and of Samuel's sons as if some were worse in God's sight than others were. The author of First Samuel provides details concerning the two sets of sons in a way that advances the ongoing story. Eli's sons' sins lead to their deaths and the subsequent death of Eli—also part of the story establishing Samuel as primary figure instead of Eli. There is continuity when Samuel's sons also are wicked, but that serves a different purpose in the story, leading to the people's asking for a king since the sons are unfit to follow in a dynastic way after Samuel's death.

We humans inevitably rank sins with some worse than others—usually in a manner that makes us look better and others appear more sinful. God does not let us off the hook so easily, however. Jesus tells us that we are to love God with all our heart, soul, strength and mind, and to love our neighbors as ourselves. Not one of us does that, and we need regularly to tell God that we are truly sorry and that we humbly repent. Paul tells us that we all have sinned, and that we all continue to come short of God's glory (Romans 3:23).

There finally are but two choices—either we measure up or we do not. And not one of us does. The good news is that God loves sinners, that Jesus died for sinners, and—If we will admit the reality about our condition—that we may claim those truths as our very own.

Q **When you sin and go to God for forgiveness, do you have to tell anybody else?**

A No. "If we confess our sins, He is faithful and righteous to forgive us our sins and to cleanse us from all unrighteousness" (1 John 1:9).

Q **Will God punish us for sin even though He has forgiven us?**

A No, He does not punish for condemnation those whom He has forgiven. To the woman caught in adultery Jesus said, "...*I do not condemn you, either. Go. From now on sin no more*" (John 8:11).

God may allow you to experience the resulting consequences of *your* sin. If a friend discovers that you have been untruthful with him, he may no longer trust you. God may allow them to treat you as untruthful even after He has forgiven you. He may not supernaturally impose a change of heart within the betrayed friend.

God may discipline you in order to reform your character, "...*My son, do not regard lightly the discipline of the Lord, Nor faint when you are reproved by Him; For those whom the Lord loves*

He disciplines... All discipline for the moment seems not to be joyful, but sorrowful; yet to those who have been trained by it, afterwards it yields the peaceful fruit of righteousness" (Hebrews 12:5-11).

Q **Does Jesus accept those who have had abortions and other sins in their life?**

A Those who were guilty of His murder, He was willing to forgive.

"Therefore let all the house of Israel know for certain that God has made Him both Lord and Christ this Jesus whom you crucified. Now when they heard this they were pierced to the heart, and said to Peter and the rest of the apostles, Brethren, what shall we do? Peter said to them, Repent, and each of you be baptized in the name of Jesus Christ for the forgiveness of your sins; and you will receive the gift of the Holy Spirit." (Acts 2:36-38).

Certainly He will forgive and receive those who repent and turn to Him. But His admonition is, *"Go and sin no more"* (John 8:11).

Q *Is participation in the lottery sinful?*

A The lottery, even the Georgia Lotto, is a form of gambling. Gambling is risking the loss of resources in an artificial, created and unnecessary scheme in an attempt to obtain that which belongs to another, without rendering equivalent constructive product (service or merchandise of equivalent value) in return.

Some will say that all of life is a gamble for it involves a risk. That may be true, but the lottery is a form of gambling wherein the risk is (1) artificial, (2) created and (3) unnecessary and through that risk one obtains what belongs to another while not providing equivalent constructive product in return. This violates the very nature of Christianity (Ephesians 4:28).

What is the motivation for gambling? Visit the bet placing station and ask the patrons to contribute toward a "worthy cause." Will they? No! Obviously, they do not gamble because they wish to contribute to the cause.

Visit the bet placing station and ask the patrons to contribute to you. Will they? No! Obviously they do not gamble because they wish you or the "worthy cause" to have their funds. Therefore, gambling is not a contribution to a worthy cause.

Where does the money that the winners receive come from? It is the money that previously belonged to the losers.

What happens when you win the bet? You receive the loser's money. The loser did not want you to have his money; yet you received his money without giving the loser equivalent constructive product in exchange.

Think about that! Winners receive the loser's money and return no constructive product. Losers did not want winners to have their money.

Elsewhere in society when someone obtains your resources without giving you a constructive product, we call it cheating. Or if I receive your resources without your consent, we call it stealing (Ephesians 4:28). Even legalized gambling is inconsistent with Christianity.

If I gamble with you, I treat you in a manner in which I do not want you to treat me; for, I do not want you to have my money (Matthew 7:12). Therefore legalized gambling is inconsistent with Christianity.

Gambling promotes the spirit of obtaining something for nothing (2 Thessalonians 3:6-10). Therefore legalized gambling is inconsistent with Christianity.

Remove the element of potential gain and then let folk participate in the scheme. How many would still participate in the gambling scheme without the potential for gain? Few to none. Greed is the spirit that motivates gambling. Therefore legalized gambling is inconsistent with Christianity.

If the gambling venture gives away $2,000,000, those who gambled could have pooled their resources, produced a company, provided jobs and lost $2,000,000, thus providing a much better service to society. Gambling is an extremely poor use of resources. Gambling does not promote good stewardship.

Our Lord provided for that through taxes and benevolence (Luke 20:25, Romans 13:6-7, 2 Corinthians 9).

What about the stock market? The Stock Market is different from this gambling because investors, by purchasing stock, lend their money to the company that sells the stock. If the company makes a profit, it returns a portion of the profits to the stockholders. Or the value of the stockholder's ownership increases—all things being equal. When all is not equal, swindlers rip off investors. Honest investors cannot be charged with that treason. Therefore the stock market:

(1) is not an unnecessary risk.

(2) provides constructive product.

Christians should refuse to participate in the gambling schemes.

Q *Is it against God's will to play the lottery even if you donate some of the money to the church?*

A Why not donate the money from gambling? Gambling is equivalent to robbery and stealing, "He who steals must steal no longer; but rather he must labor, performing with his own hands what is good, so that he will have something to share with one who has need" (Ephesians 4:28). What you do with the proceeds do not validate how you got it.

Q *I have been dating a guy for six years and have engaged in sex periodically. I did not feel right about it and stopped for about 1 1/2 years. If he gives me a ring and we set a date, is it okay to*

engage in sex at that point? What constitutes marriage in God's eyes (is it the commitment, the ring or the marriage)?

A No, it is not okay with God to engage in premarital sex. Therefore, I commend you for abstaining from premarital sexual intercourse for 1 1/2 years while dating. Usually, six years of dating is too long.

Regardless of which way you cut it, it still slices into fornication. God offers His remedy. *"Now concerning the things about which you wrote, it is good for a man not to touch a woman. But because of immoralities, each man is to have his own wife, and each woman is to have her own husband. The husband must fulfill his duty to his wife, and likewise also the wife to her husband. The wife does not have authority over her own body, but the husband does and likewise also the husband does not have authority over his own body, but the wife does"* (1 Corinthians 7:1-4).

Marriage is a bilateral covenant between a man and a woman. A covenant is a determined and ratified agreement. To become married, a man and a woman must be committed to be married and express that commitment to each other. *"So the Lord God caused a deep sleep to fall upon the man, and he slept; then He took one of his ribs and closed up the flesh at that place. The Lord God fashioned into a woman the rib which He had taken from the man, and brought her to the man. The man said, This is now bone of my bones, And flesh of my flesh; She shall be called Woman, Because she was taken out of Man. For this reason a man shall leave his father and his mother, and be joined to his wife; and they shall become one flesh. And the man and his wife were both naked and were not ashamed"* (Genesis 2:21-25).

Without commitment, each partner, like a commissioned salesman, is on trial charged to produce a pleasing performance each day.. Think of living with someone who does not love and trust you enough to make a commitment to continue to love you after the heat of passion has cooled and real-life problems begin to develop. If a person pledges love where there is none, promises lifelong commitment without intention, there would be serious question as to whether a valid marriage has been formed. Scriptures offer no precedent or instruction for a formal wedding ceremony. However by His presence, Jesus endorsed the public wedding ceremony (John 2:1-2).

Q **Is it okay to move in a week in advance of the actual marriage ceremony if no sex is involved?**

A No. Be careful that lustful thoughts are restrained. Generally I advise against it and explain in Premarital Counseling why it is not wise. How can you control your desire for intimacy? Why stress yourself unnecessarily?

Q *Is it wrong to have premarital sex if you are engaged?*

A Yes. Until one is married, he or she is not married. Sex before marriage is sin (1 Corinthians 7:1-2, 1 Corinthians 6:9-11).

Q *I am a born-again Christian. I am not married, but we have been living together for years. It is now beginning to bother me. What should I do?*

A Depart (1 Corinthians 6:9-11) or marry (1 Corinthians 7:1-2).

Q *Why would a person become gay?*

A Homosexual practices are contrary to the will of God, evidenced by the fact that God gave them up, *"For since the creation of the world His invisible attributes, His eternal power and divine nature, have been clearly seen, being understood through what has been made, so that they are without excuse. For even though they knew God, they did not honor Him as God or give thanks, but they became futile in their speculations, and their foolish heart was darkened. Professing to be wise, they became fools, and exchanged the glory of the incorruptible God for an image in the form of corruptible man and of birds and four-footed animals and crawling creatures. Therefore, God gave them over in the lusts of their hearts to impurity, so that their bodies would be dishonored among them.*

For they exchanged the truth of God for a lie, and worshiped and served the creature rather than the Creator, who is blessed forever. Amen. For this reason God gave them over to degrading passions; for their women exchanged the natural function for that which is unnatural, and in the same way also the men abandoned the natural function of the woman and burned in their desire toward one another, men with men committing indecent acts and receiving in their own persons the due penalty of their error. And just as they did not see fit to acknowledge God any longer, God gave them over to a depraved mind, to do those things which are not proper" (Romans 1:20-27).

Q Where in the Bible does it speak on homosexuality? Is it normal to be attracted to the same sex?

A The Scripture that relates to homosexuality is Romans 1:20-27. No, homosexuality is unnatural, *"For since the creation of the world His invisible attributes, His eternal power and divine nature, have been clearly seen, being understood through what has been made, so that they are without excuse. For even though they knew God, they did not honor Him as God or give thanks, but they became futile in their speculations, and their foolish heart was darkened. Professing to be wise, they became fools, and exchanged the glory of the incorruptible God for an image in the form of corruptible man and of birds and four-footed animals and crawling creatures. Therefore, God gave them over in the lusts of their hearts to impurity, so that their bodies would be dishonored among them. For they exchanged the truth of God for a lie, and worshiped and served the creature rather than the Creator, who is blessed forever. Amen. For this reason God gave them over to degrading passions; for their women exchanged the natural function for that which is unnatural, and in the same way also the men abandoned the natural function of the woman and burned in their desire toward one another, men with men committing indecent acts and receiving in their own persons the due penalty of their error. And just as they did not see fit to acknowledge God any longer, God gave them over to a depraved mind, to do those things which are not proper"* (Romans 1:20-27).

Q **I have been involved in the homosexual experience, but have been born-again. Now the urge to involve myself in the homosexual experience is very strong. How can I actually overcome the urge?**

A Resist the urge: 1 Peter 5:7, Ephesians 6:12-17.

Q **Where in the Bible does it state that suicide is sin?**

A Suicide is murder. *"You shall not murder"* (Exodus 20:13).

"For this, "You shall not commit adultery, You shall not murder, You shall not steal, You shall not covet," and if there is any other commandment, it is summed up in this saying, "You shall love your neighbor as yourself." (Romans 13:9)

For He who said, "Do not commit adultery," also said, "Do not commit murder." Now if you do not commit adultery, but do commit murder, you have become a transgressor of the law. (James 2:11)

Q ***What does the Bible say about suicide? How can I help someone who is considering suicide? How can I lead them back to the Lord?***

A God gave and gives life (Genesis 2:7). Only at His request should life be taken. Through Scripture, God expresses His value of human life. We ought to adopt His view and seek to preserve life. Refer them to a licensed counselor for professional therapeutic help. Discover what led them away from the Lord. Remind them that they do have hope (Romans 6:17-18, 2 Corinthians 4:8-18).

Q ***Do people who commit suicide go to hell?***

A I Do not know. Is someone responsible for behavior when he loses rational thinking ability? Some suicides may take place after one has lost his mind.

Q Is playing and hearing rap music a sin?

A The style and category of music has little influence upon our thinking and behavior. However, the lyrics of music do influence our thinking and behavior. We should never underestimate the power of music even when we are unaware. When we allow rap or any other type of music to influence us toward sin, it then becomes sinful. We must remember 1 Corinthians 15:33. Even when no sin is involved, one may be wise to not aggravate his soul with unnecessary vile suggestions (2 Peter 2:4-9). Chose between better and best.

Q Is it okay to drink wine with your dinner?

A God demands that we be sober, *"so then let us not sleep as others do, but let us be alert and sober"* (1 Thessalonians 5:6).

"The end of all things is near; therefore, be of sound judgment and sober spirit for the purpose of prayer" (1 Peter 4:7). Does this interfere with soberness?

God demands that we not place a stumbling block in the way of weak believers, *"Do not tear down the work of God for the sake of food. All things indeed are clean, but they are evil for the man who eats and gives offense. It is good not to eat meat or to drink wine, or to do anything by which your brother stumbles"* (Romans 14:20-21).

Does this destroy your soberness and may it cause weak believers to stumble?

Q *What should I do? My spouse has a drinking problem and refuses to seek help. She has become physically abusive.*

A Jesus separated Himself from those who were attempting to do Him bodily harm (Matthew 12:14-16; John 8:59; 10:31, 39-40; 11:53-57).

Q *How does a saved person overcome the sin of drug addiction?*

A You overcome the sin of drug addiction like you would every other type of addiction. You must decide to overcome and employ strategies that will help. The apostle Paul said it best, *"Therefore I urge you, brethren, by the mercies of God, to present your bodies a living and holy sacrifice, acceptable to God, which is your spiritual service of worship. And do not be conformed to this world, but be transformed by the renewing of your mind, so that you may prove what the will of God is, that which is good and acceptable and perfect"* (Romans 12:1-2).

Q *My husband is on drugs. Are we really supposed to be one? Is the man supposed to be the head of the household?*

A Drugs are unfortunately a devastating element. No family has been immunized against their influence. It is difficult to function as one with someone who is failing to cooperate. He should be the head, but obviously is not functioning as the head (Ephesians 5:23, 25-28; 6:4).

Q *Does cigarette smoke jeopardize one's discipleship?*

A Discipleship has to do with one's service to the Lord. Smoking may interfere with one's acceptance. The Bible never directly addresses the right or wrong of smoking.

Q *Is it a sin to play bingo?*

A Likely, the exact format of bingo playing varies from time to time and from place to place. I am unaware of those specifics. However, everywhere in society when a person obtains another's resources, gives him nothing of constructive value in return, and the previous owner did not want him to have his resources, we call it stealing and/or robbery. Why then do we not call it stealing and/or robbery when the scheme is the same, but the government sanctions it? The state never decides morality. Jehovah God our creator dictates the standard of morality. God says, He who steals must steal no longer; but rather he must labor, performing with his own hands what is good, so that he will have something to share with one who has need" (Ephesians 4:28).

Death

God set life and death before Adam. He warned Adam that death would result from disobedience to His Word (Genesis 2:16-17). When Adam disobeyed God, he chose death over life. After sin, death became an unalterable decree of God (Genesis 3:22-24; Hebrews 9:27).

Death reduces every person to a common level (Genesis 5:5, 8, 11, 14, 17, 20, 27, 31). But Scripture reveals that God will resurrect the physical bodies of His people from the dead. For the people of God, death is only a transition into a more grand and glorious lifestyle. Because of the resurrection, death is a new beginning.

Q What is death?

A First, we need to know what life is. Life is the unification of spirit with the body (Genesis 1:26-27, 2:7). Death is the opposite, the separation of the spirit from the body (James. 2:26, Luke 23:46).

Q How do you know what happens to you after death?

A The Scripture argues for a resurrection of the body (1 Corinthians 15:12-49). More than once it argues for a resurrection, *"For the Lord Himself will descend from heaven with a shout, with the voice of the archangel and with the trumpet of God, and the dead in Christ will rise first"* (1 Thessalonians 4:16).

Q When we die, where does our soul immediately go?

A Death is the separating of the spirit and body (James 2:26). When one dies, the spirit returns to God (Ecclesiastes 12:7). When Jesus was at the point of death, He understood that God would receive His spirit (Luke 23:46) and Stephen (Acts 7:59) and the apostle Paul (2 Corinthians 5:6-8) did as well.

Q What happens when we die?

A First, we need to know who we are while we are alive. We are a spirit, who inhabits a body and possesses a soul (1 Thessalonians 5:23, Hebrews 4:12).

When we die:

(1) our spirit returns to God (Luke 23:46, Acts 7:59, 2 Corinthians 5:6-9).

(2) our body returns to the earth (Genesis. 3:19, Job 34:14-15, Ecclesiastes 12:7).

Which gets more attention, the spirit or body?

Q *What happens after the wicked dies?*

A (1) Those who die unforgiven of sin, unsaved and lost will ultimately be raised to condemnation (John 5:28-29, 8:24, 21, Romans 8:1-2).

(2) Those who die unforgiven of sin, unsaved and lost will ultimately be banished from the presence of God (2 Thessalonians 1:6-9).

(3) Those who die unforgiven of sin, unsaved and lost will ultimately be thrown into the lake of fire (Matthew 13:4-42, Revelations 20:11-15, 21:8).

What should you now do? Obey God, become forgiven (Acts 2:38) be saved (Mark 16:16). Live a life of faith.

Q *What happens after the righteous dies?*

A (1) Those who die forgiven of sin, and saved will ultimately be raised to life everlasting (John 5:28-29, Romans 8:1-2).

(2) Those that die forgiven of sin, and saved will ultimately be bashing in the eternal presence of God (1 Thessalonians 4:16-18).

(3) Those that die forgiven of sin, and saved will ultimately be enjoying their inheritance (Revelations 21:1-7).

What should you now do? Obey God, become forgiven (Acts 2:38) be saved (Mark 16:16). Live a life of faith.

MARRIAGE

Reflecting upon His creation, God saw that it was good (Genesis 1:4; 10; 12; 18; 21; 25; 31). But when He saw the loneliness of Adam, He said that it was not good (Genesis 2:18). Did God speak correctly when He said it was not for man to be alone? Whatever God says is good is good, but what God says is not good is certainly not good.

Why was Adam's loneliness not good? God instilled within Adam an inherent need for male and female human beings to relate to each other. Neither the animal kingdom nor the plant kingdom could satisfy Adam's aloneness. Adam needed a wife.

We have the same needs as did Adam (Matthew 19:10; 1 Corinthians 7:9). Through marriage we can satisfy our human relationship needs better than through anything else.

Q *What is marriage? And, when is a person married?*

A Marriage is a God-witnessed bilateral covenant for social and physical intercourse between a man and a woman for life (Genesis 2:18-; 22-25; Matthew 19:3-6).

Two people are married when they covenant (commit to be married). The basis for marriage is a social covenant, not just a legal agreement. Never does God say one word about marriage being a legal arrangement, but He defines it as social.

Q *What constitutes "being married"? Is a private commitment a marriage? Is a ceremony needed? Is it the sexual relationship that makes marriage? Does the Bible speak to these issues?*

A Sex outside of marriage is fornication (12 Corinthians 7:1-4). Marriage is a bilateral covenant between a man and a woman (Genesis 2:21-25). A covenant is a determined and ratified agreement. To become married, a man and a woman must be committed to be married and express that commitment to each other.

If a person pledges love where there is none, promises lifelong commitment without intention, there would be serious question as to whether a valid marriage has been formed.

Scriptures offer no precedent or instruction for a formal wedding ceremony. However by His presence, Jesus endorsed the public wedding ceremony (John 2:1-2).

Q *Who is ready to marry?*

A Marriage is for adults who can leave their father and mother and bond emotionally with a spouse. These adults must be willing to share innermost thoughts and feelings with each other. Individuals who are so attached to others that they cannot relinquish and responsibly bond with their mates are unprepared for marriage. Marriage is for the mature.

Q *What does it mean for a man to leave father and mother and be joined to his wife (Genesis 2:24; Matthew 19:5)? Does that mean that a married man cannot live in the house with his parents?*

A Marriage is a social bonding covenant. When two people marry, they form a social bonding covenant with each other that supercedes the previous social bond with their parents. This superceding social bonding covenant can be maintained while living in the house with parents. Scripture never mandates leaving the physical domain of parents when marrying. However, if remaining in the parents' home interferes with the husband and wife bonding, then moving would definitely be a necessity.

Q *What are some indicators that one may be mature enough to marry?*

A Those who have the:
   (1) ability to remain with a job

(2) capacity to be reliable

(3) ability and willingness to give more on any job than is asked for

(4) persistence to carry out plans despite the difficulty

(5) ability to work with others within an organization and under authority

(6) ability to make decisions

(7) will to live

(8) flexibility, independence and tolerance needed to succeed.

Q *Why does so much conflict exist within marriage?*

A Often conflict occurs because of incorrect information and insufficient information provided to potential married partners. Conflict exists within every marital relationship. It is not if conflict will occur but, when conflict will occur. Conflict occurs when a person must choose between two compelling and repelling demands. However, our marital relationships can exist with a minimal (manageable) amount of conflict. Awareness of the phases of conflict will help us to regulate and manage our conflict.

The first phase of conflict is the **nuisance phase,** the intense "discussing phase." At this phase you feel that your spouse occasionally interferes with your ultimate happiness. However, both of you continue to tolerate each other both physically and emotionally. During this phase, you neither intentionally retaliate physically nor emotionally. In other words, you wish your spouse would... but when your spouse does not, you remain physically and emotionally connected.

The second phase of conflict within the marital relationship is the **hindrance phase,** the intense "fussing phase." At this phase you feel that your spouse frequently interferes with your ultimate happiness. However, you continue to physically tolerate each other. But, one or maybe both of you refuse to emotionally tolerate the other. You suppress physical retaliation to a minimum, but you allow emotional retaliation to escalate. In other words, you wish your spouse would, and when your spouse does not, you remain physically connected, but emotionally you disconnect from the other.

Did you notice that emotional conflict preceded physical conflict? Emotional conflict may be more devastating than physical conflict.

The third stage of conflict is the **threat phase**. I call this the "cussing phase." You have left the "discussing" phase and gone beyond the "fussing" phase. At this phase, you feel that your spouse always interferes with your ultimate happiness.

Retaliation increases. You neither physically nor emotionally tolerate your spouse. In other words, you wish your spouse would, but when your spouse does not, you withdraw both physically and emotionally.

Q *How can I reduce the conflict?*
A We can learn adequate behavior from adequate models.

First, find seven Christian couples who share **polite conversation** with each other and model after them. Listen to how couples talk to each other and select only the ones who are polite to each other.

Second, find seven Christian couples who share **personal chemistry** with each other and model after them. Look for spouses who bring a "sparkle" to the eye of each other just by their presence.

Third, find seven Christian couples who share **problem-solving conscience** and model after them. Discover their strategies. Within the marital relationship, conflict is inevitable. Therefore, you need to commit yourself to learn how to solve conflict-producing problems.

Q *Where in the Bible does it say he who finds a wife finds a good thing?*
A "He who finds a wife finds a good thing And obtains favor from the Lord" (Proverbs 18:22).

Q *Where in the Bible does it say that a man and a woman should be married? Where does it say that a man should have only one wife?*
A Read 1 Corinthians 7:1-2.

Q *How do you know when God sends you a soul mate?*

A If God sends a soul mate, He would want you to know. Therefore, somehow God would tell you. Nothing in Scripture suggests that God is going to directly send you a soul mate.

Q *Should a single Christian woman date at all or wait for God to supply a mate?*

A God knows two categories of persons: 1) the unmarried without commitment and 2) the married with commitment. God knows no in between stage. God never sanctions being in a dating relationship just for dating and romance sakes (1 Timothy 5:1-2).

We do discover a relationship developing that is leading to marriage (Matthew 1:18-18-20, Luke 1:26-27). However while dating to marry, one needs to remain uncommitted and behave as if unmarried (1 Timothy 4:11-5:2).

Actively one may date to discover a compatible mate. Passively one may wait to be discovered by a compatible mate.

Q *If while going to premarital counseling, we disagree on money, personal time, and responsibilities, should we postpone the marriage?*

A Generally Premarital Preparations help answer two questions, (1) What is your relationship like right now? (2) What changes will be most helpful for you to implement as you plan for a lifelong commitment to your spouse?

A. You may discover that your relationship right now fails to provide a healthy foundation for developing a lifelong commitment within marriage. If so, you may decide to postpone the sessions, and end the dating relationship. Or, you may continue to date, but make changes that bring a greater degree of healthiness to the relationship.
B. You may discover that your relationship right now provides a healthy foundation for developing a lifelong commitment within marriage. Keep dating and proceed with premarital preparations.
C. You may discover that the different views about money, personal time, and responsibilities demand more changes within the marriage than you are willing to make. End the dating and premarital preparations, and move on elsewhere with life.
D. You may discover that the different views about money, personal time and responsibilities demand changes that you are willing to make. Begin to adjust your attitude, prepare to make them, keep dating, and continue with premarital preparations.
E. All of these options are also true for your prospective spouse.

Q *I have been married for one year. For the past six months, my husband has been on drugs and has been unfaithful, and neglectful as a father. How long should I give him to get his life back together?*

A Marriage is a commitment. You committed to be married. Only you can decide to no longer be committed. You just have to decide how long you will wait for your husband to be restored to his commitment. No one else can decide for you.

Remember that unfaithfulness and drug usage often introduces child neglect and abuse, spousal abuse, AIDS, hepatitis, and other illnesses. However, I would suggest that you look for indicators that your husband is going to return to his commitment. The more indicators that you see, the longer you may wait. The fewer indicators that you see, the shorter time you may wait. Above all, I recommend making an appointment to see your therapeutic minister (spiritual advisor) or a reputable counselor immediately.

Q *I married, unaware that the man was already married. He has since divorced his first wife. We have not remarried. How does God look upon my marriage?*

A You did not form a legal marriage union when you thought you married your husband. Our law prohibits polygamy. The man that you intended to marry was not available to marry you.

Therefore, no marriage took place. He deceived you. You were not married then and you are not married now.

Q *Is it a sin to marry or stay with the brother or father of my deceased husband and let him help raise children fathered by deceased man?*

A It is honorable for your children's uncle and grandfather to help raise your children in the death of your husband. Nothing within Scripture prohibits you from marrying whoever is presently unmarried.

Q *How can I get my spouse interested in becoming a Christian?*

A Your Christian behavior increases your probabilities to their greatest level.

Jesus informed us. *"Let your light shine before men in such a way that they may see your good works, and glorify your Father who is in heaven"* (Matthew 5:16).

The apostle Peter informed us. *"In the same way, you wives, be submissive to your own husbands so that even if any of them are disobedient to the word, they may be won without a word by the behavior of their wives, as they observe your chaste and respectful behavior"* (1 Peter 3:1-2).

Q *What should a person do if the husband isn't doing what it takes to be head of the household?*

A Each spouse should always fulfill the responsibilities God expects regardless of what his spouse does or doesn't do. More specifically, address the reason why your spouse is failing.

Is your spouse failing because of lack of information? If so, inform them. You may do this personally, through counseling, couples groups, Bible study, or another influential person.

Is your spouse failing because of lack of integrity? If so rebuke him. In the latter case, the probability of helping him is much less.

Q *What does the Bible require of us regarding second marriages?*

A It requires the same principles for the second as for first. The Bible emphasizes how to remain married in the first one (Ephesians 5:22).

Q *I am contemplating marriage, but I am divorced. My boyfriend is having a hard time dealing with my divorce status. What should I do?*

A Cancel the wedding plans. End your dating relationship with him. Never enter a marriage with unresolved notions about previous relationships or present status. If both cannot marry without annoying reservations, do not do it.

Q *Is it wrong to remarry my ex-husband? Was it a mistake to divorce him?*

A No (1 Corinthians 7:10-11). The Old Testament passages that address marrying one's previously divorced spouse does prohibit it after they had married someone else (Deuteronomy 24:1-4).

Q *What does the Bible say about physical abuse within marriage?*

A Through principles of Scripture, God sought to create comfortable marriage relationships. Each husband is told to love his wife as he loves himself. Each wife is told to submit to her husband (Ephesians 5:22-33; Colossians 3:18-19; 1 Peter 3:1-7). When Biblical principles are followed, physical and every other type of abuse will cease.

DIVORCE

Too often spouses suppose that marriage will be a continuation of their past romantic and highly sexualized courtship—and at the same time meet their needs for emotional nurture, social interchange and belonging identity. They expect their mates to make them feel whole and happy. Unfulfilled expectations erode their commitment to remain married.

Even though decreased social, moral and legal restraints have relaxed our cultural attitudes toward the permanence of marriage, it is an unwillingness to continue their commitment to their marriage vows that finalizes the divorce proceedings.

Moses allowed a Hebrew man to divorce his wife for the uncleanliness or indecency of the wife (Deuteronomy 24:1-4). There exists a diversity of opinions as to the meaning of uncleanliness. Very likely the charge was something other than fornication because capital punishment was the penalty for such (Leviticus 20:10).

The legal action of divorce that ends the marital relationship is different from the behavior that warranted the divorce (indecency and hardness of heart). The funeral does not kill the corpse—it just buries it. Divorce does not kill the marriage—it just buries it.

Divorce is just a symbol of the sin that severs the marital relationship between a husband and a wife. The behavior that caused the deterioration that led to the divorce is the real problem.

Q Explain Matthew 19:8-9

A Jesus is clarifying the principles of the law of Moses. An earlier mention of divorce and marrying will help us (Deuteronomy 24:1-4). Therefore, it was not just divorce, but the subsequent marrying again that permanently severed the first marriage. Therefore, Jesus explained that divorcing and marrying constituted adultery (Matthew 19:8-9). Sex with the new wife is not what constituted adultery.

Adultery was to contaminate or violate a covenant. Marriage is a covenant.

Further help will be to consider that the Pharisees came testing (tempting) Jesus (Matthew 19:3). Normally Jesus did not provide a comprehensive explanation for insincere people. So we should not think that Matthew

19 contains God's comprehensive and complete instruction about marriage to the elimination of other passages of Scripture. However, He indicated that God intended for the marriage covenant to be permanent (Matthew 19:4-6).

Further help will be to notice the real question. The question was can a married man divorce, not can a divorced person marry. Let's follow the principles of Jesus and elevate marriages to the level that God intended (Hebrews 13:4 – 1; Peter 1:19; 2 Peter 1:4).

Q Does Romans 7:2-4 sanction divorce?

A. No. *"Or do you not know, brethren (for I am speaking to those who know the law), that the law has jurisdiction over a person as long as he lives? For the married woman is bound by law to her husband while he is living; but if her husband dies, she is released from the law concerning the husband. So then, if while her husband is living she is joined to another man, she shall be called an adulteress; but if her husband dies, she is free from the law, so that she is not an adulteress though she is joined to another man. Therefore, my brethren, you also were made to die to the Law through the body of Christ, so that you might be joined to another, to Him who was raised from the dead, in order that we might bear fruit for God"* (Romans 7:1-4). God uses "a" truth about marriage to illustrate "a" truth about the law.

Q What does "put away " in 1 Corinthians 7:11 mean?
A It means divorce because the person becomes unmarried.

Q Why not just divorce when conflict mounts?
A God hates divorce (Malachi 2:16; Genesis 2:22). Divorce is too expensive.

Q How expensive is divorce?
A Divorce costs the community. It deprives the community of the example of an enduring marital commitment. Also, divorce destroys the notion of permanence in marriage and fuels the false notion that everyone is divorcing. Divorce divides the social circle. Frequently, the divorced couple refuses to allow close friends to remain friends with both. Being a friend to one former spouse alienates from the other.

Divorce costs the children economically. Frequently, the children become the custody of the mother. One survey showed that mothers suffered a 71 percent decrease in spendable income while the fathers enjoyed a 43 percent increase in spendable income.

Divorce costs the children emotionally. Every child progresses better within a healthy two-parent emotional environment. The divorce of their parents provides emotional baggage that haunts the children even within their own marriage relationships.

Divorce depresses the children's ego. They lose status as they become step-brothers and step-sisters. Their vulnerability toward abuse and incest increases.

Divorce costs the couple emotionally. There really is no such thing as divorce in the absolute sense of the term. Marriage involves a reciprocal and irrevocable investment of lives. That relationship may be altered, but can never cease to exist. You may divide the property, but never can go back to being single. Often couples are alarmed at the intensity of their relationship.

Divorce costs energetically. Even after divorcing, both parents still have full parental responsibility to raise their children. The energy needed to raise children after divorcing, if invested during the marriage, could have managed the conflict and kept the marriage intact.

If we believe that God knows best, then we must admit that God's ideal, a two-parent family, provides positives that unmarried parents simply cannot provide. Or, we must admit that God gave us the inferior family system.

But, someone will say, "You do not understand the intensity of my pain in this marriage." Some surveys show that only 10 percent of the time do both divorced former spouses say they find fulfillment after divorcing. Divorce then has a 90 percent failure rate, twice the failure rate for marriage.

Problems experienced by those who divorce are not greater than the problems experienced by those who remain married. Those who divorce renege on their commitment while those who remain married do not.

Usually divorce is too expensive. Before you divorce, calculate all the costs. The known costs plus the unknown costs may just be more than you can afford to pay.

Q *I have just been served divorce papers. What can I do if I do not want the divorce?*

A Refuse to sign the papers. See if you can get a commitment from your spouse to work to reconcile the relationship. If you can, then find a marriage counselor to help. If you cannot get a commitment from your spouse to work to reconcile the relationship, why would you want to remain married to someone who wishes not to remain married to you?

Q *I just filed for a divorce. My husband was released from prison in 1989 and is back in jail now. He started doing things that I did not approve of. Should I continue with the divorce or should I reconcile?*

A No one else can make the decision about divorce for you. Seriously consider the probability of reconciling and developing a healthy marriage relationship.

Q *If a wife is caught in adultery and her husband forgives her, can he hold the adultery against her later and use it to get a divorce?*

A Forgiveness and proceeding as if the offense never happened are two separate issues. Forgiveness means that we view them as no longer being guilty of the offense; however, there may be lingering consequences for the offensive behavior.

Jesus allowed not commanded, divorce when adultery had been committed. Everywhere within Scripture, Jesus commanded that we forgive. We cannot understand that He was allowing divorce only when the spouse had not forgiven the other. Therefore, it is possible to forgive, but to also divorce the guilty spouse. God forgave Moses but refused to allow him to enter the Promised Land. He forgave David, yet refused to allow him to build the temple.

Q *When a husband has left the marriage, by law what can be done? He is living in another house and has started another family without getting a divorce.*

A Contact an attorney. If a spouse persists to destroy his marriage covenant, the marriage is positioned to become null and void. Before you make the covenant, you have no marriage. After you have destroyed the covenant, you have no marriage.

Q *Should I divorce my husband who is now staying with another person?*

A Marriage is a covenant commitment to provide social intercourse. It is good that the legal system of our society recognizes and sanctions marriage. However from its beginning, marriage was a covenant between a man and a woman with God to provide social companionship.

God instituted marriage to solve a "not good aloneness", "Then the Lord God said, *"It is not good for the man to be alone; I will make him a helper suitable for him"* (Genesis 2:18). Therefore, God provided a wife for Adam, *"The Lord God fashioned into a woman the rib which He had taken from the man, and brought her to the man"* (Genesis 2:22).

If your husband is refusing to honor his covenant commitment, he has divorced you socially. You are the only person who can decide how long you are willing to wait for him to return to his covenant commitment. You just have to make a decision. The Bible does not prohibit you from allowing the legal system of our society to recognize that you are divorced.

Q *If a husband is a substance abuser, should the wife stay in the marriage or seek a divorce?*

A Each husband and wife should work toward compatibility and comfort. Marriage is a social covenant. When a spouse constantly violates their covenant, the other spouse has to decide to what extent he/she will patiently wait for the wayward spouse to return to their covenant agreement. When a spouse has reneged on their covenant commitment, he has thereby deserted the marriage.

Q *My husband was severely injured in an accident. He is mentally and physically challenged. What should I do about our marriage? I know the Bible says through sickness and health. Can I get a divorce?*

A The Bible never says the vows. That is your commitment. Why would you even consider abandoning him? What should he do if you had been in the accident?

Q *Would it be Biblical to divorce a spouse that no longer desires sexual intercourse?*

A No, God hates both the divorce and the disposition of heart that brings about divorce (Malachi 2:16, Matthew 19:8-9). Marriage is more than just a union for sexual intercourse. Marriage is a covenant for companionship for life (Genesis 2:18-25). It would be far better to seek to discover the cause and cure for the loss of interest rather than divorce.

Q *My ex-husband divorced me, remarried, but is yet alive. Is it okay for me to remarry?*

A It seems that you are presently unmarried. If all other things are equal, I see no reason in

Scripture that prevents you from marrying. *"Are you bound to a wife? Do not seek to be released. Are you released from a wife? Do not seek a wife. But if you marry, you have not sinned; and if a virgin marries, she has not sinned. Yet such will have trouble in this life, and I am trying to spare you"* (1 Corinthians 7:27-28).

Q I have been married and divorced three times. What does the Lord say?

A Marriage is a covenant between a man and a woman for life (Genesis 2:22-24). He also says the divorcing and marrying constitutes adultery (Matthew 19:9). Now that you have sinned, God will forgive (1 John 1:6-2:2).

Q How does the Bible address step-parenting? I'm recently divorced. My wife remarried and her new husband says I must request to see my son through him. His mother refuses to talk to me.

A You are not a step-parent. You are a parent. Why do you not have custody of your son? In many instances, fathers need to demand a hearing and obtain custody of their children. Then bring them up in the nurture and admonition of the Lord (Ephesians 6:1-4). It is past time for men to roll over and allow the court system and ex-wives to take their children and create chaos.

But for your situation, I ask are his restrictions unrealistic? If not, abide by them, for he is the male parent on location. If his restrictions are unrealistic, attempt to negotiate with him. If no concessions are made, revisit the judicial system for changes.

Things That You Should Do

Because of and by the blood of Jesus, you can become forgiven of sin. The blood of Christ cleanses you from the guilt of sin as you are born into the family of God. Only through Jesus Christ can you enjoy a saved relationship with God. Jesus declared that He was the only way to the Father (John 14:6).

Hear

In Jesus Christ salvation, deliverance from the penalty of sin, is available for you (John 6:44-45). You must hear the gospel, the good news that Jesus Christ has become the sacrifice for your sin (1 Corinthians 15:1-4).

The book of Acts contains many conversion stories. Preceding each conversion, the disciples preached Jesus Christ and Him crucified to the lost audience (Acts 2:36, 8:5, 35).

Believe

For the gospel to benefit you, you must believe the message (Acts 15:7). Unless you believe, you will never become converted (Hebrews 4:1-2).

Repent

Repent, change your mind, purpose, opinion, moral thought, reflection and attitude (Acts 17:30; Luke 13:3-5).

Confess

The word "confess" means to acknowledge, admit, or agree with. You must agree with God that indeed Jesus Christ is His Son (Acts 8:37).

Become Baptized

Baptism is your burial in water in response to your faith in Jesus Christ as the Son of God (Acts 8:12, 37-39; 1 Peter 3:21). Jesus placed salvation after baptism (Mark 16:16). Near the beginning and the ending of his ministry, the apostle Peter taught that baptism was inherently connected to salvation (Acts 2:38, 1 Peter 3:21).

About the Author

John Marshall has given more than 2,000 presentations throughout the United States, helping thousands of people with his practical and penetrating teaching style. He is an author, editor, media producer, facilitator for conflict resolution, motivational speaker, preacher, public relations director, teacher, trainer, and relationship consultant. He received his bachelor's degree from Freed-Hardeman University, master's degree in counseling from Theological University of America, and has done additional graduate work at University of Memphis and Southern Christian University. He is a staff writer for *The Christian Echo* and *The Revivalist* magazine, a member of the Alumni Advisory Board of Freed-Hardeman University, and preaches for Graceview Church of Christ in Stone Mountain, Georgia, where he and his family live.

Other Books by John Marshall

Good and Angry
A Personal Guide to Anger Management

God Knows!
There Is No Need to Worry

God, Listen!
Prayers That God Always Answers
(includes addiction-recovery guide)

My God !
Who He Is Will Change Your Life

The Power of the Tongue
What You Say Is What You Get

Success Is a God Idea

Show Me the Money
7 Exercises That Build Economic Strength

Contact Information

For further information about John Marshall, his ministry, and other ministry resources, please contact him at

Mail:
John Marshall
P. O. Box 878
Pine Lake Georgia 30072

Web:
www.graceview.us

Email:
jdm@graceview.us

Phone:
(404) 297-9050
(404) 316-5525

www.ingramcontent.com/pod-product-compliance
Lightning Source LLC
Chambersburg PA
CBHW031252290426
44109CB00012B/547